FOR A
LITTLE GIRL

No Job
for a
Little Girl

Voices from Domestic Service

ROSEMARY SCADDEN

To
Louisa and Joanna

It is the custom of 'Society' to abuse its servants – a façon de parler, *such as leads their lords and masters to talk of the weather, and, when rurally inclined, of the crops, – leads matronly ladies, and ladies just entering on their probation in that honoured and honourable state, to talk of servants, and, as we are told, wax eloquent over the greatest plague in life while taking a quiet cup of tea … It is another conviction of 'Society' that the race of good servants has died out, at least in England, although they do order these things better in France; that there is neither honesty, conscientiousness, nor the careful and industrious habits which distinguished the servants of our grandmothers and great-grandmothers; that domestics no longer know their place; that the introduction of cheap silks and cottons, and still more recently, those ambiguous 'materials' and tweeds, have removed the landmarks between the mistress and her maid, between the master and his man.*

Mrs Beeton's *Book of Household Management* 1859–61

Acknowledgements

My biggest 'Thank You' goes to the women I interviewed all those years ago. It proved to be a timely experience. I did not want their life stories to sit unread on my book shelf and so I was determined to get them published. My second 'Thank You' therefore goes to Professor Chris Williams who was my original supervisor, in Cardiff University, and has quietly supported my endeavours. He agreed with me that the transcripts should reach a wider audience, and not just in academia. So many Welsh families have similar stories to tell and in many cases women did not share their anecdotes, believing them to be commonplace. What was ordinary becomes extraordinary with time. I have been frequently told by members of the audiences at the lectures I give, 'My mother never talked about it. She's dead now of course, so I'll never know now what her life was like and how hard it must have been for her to leave home at fourteen.'

The quotation from *Goodbye to All That* is reprinted here by permission of United Agents on behalf of: The Trustees of the Robert Graves Copyright Trust. Don Llewellyn generously gave me the licence for a male indoor servant. Dilwyn Morgan nobly allowed me use his mother's precious letter. Catrin Stevens was very quick to offer her aunt's photo when I was bemoaning the fact that such pictures were hard to find. Cameras were a rarity and why would you waste valuable film on taking a photograph of the maid! The Glamorgan Archives have played their part in allowing me use a number of documents without paying any fee. Thank you all for your kind help.

I trust that the faith, investment and work that Gomer Press has put into this venture will be well rewarded.

Rosemary Scadden
July 2013

Contents

Foreword

I am writing this foreword in my study, an attic room used just over a century ago as a bedroom by a domestic servant. Mary Thomas, born in Abercynon in about 1882, was by the time of the 1911 population census the general domestic servant in Bellnoir, Tyfica Road, Pontypridd, a good example of what the writer Alun Richards termed 'Rhondda baronial' architecture. The householder was (appropriately) architect and surveyor George Vincent Evans (then aged thirty-six), who lived at Bellnoir with his wife Jennet (thirty-one) and their nine-month-old daughter Constance Marguerite (truly a 'baronial' name). All were Glamorgan-born, and the language of the household was English, although servant Mary spoke both Welsh and English. Out of her bedroom window Mary would have been able to see the imposing edifice of Jacobsdal (named after a town in the Orange Free State, South Africa), immediately behind on the hill. In 1911 that was a large private house, but it features in this book (Anglicised as Jacobsdale) as a training academy for domestic servants in the inter-war decades. Today Jacobsdal has been replaced by the Pontypridd District Club, home of live music and equipped with two full-sized snooker tables, but the thought that trainee servants would have been able to look over the wall and into the room in which I now work is intriguing.

Neither of these connections between where I now work and the contents of this book had been anticipated before I read the stories Rosemary Scadden has so skilfully gathered together here. I did know of other links. Like many of us from South Wales I have domestic servants in my family tree. My maternal grandmother, Annie Standley – always known as 'Nancy' – born in Cwmbran in 1910, had left South Wales in about 1927 and found work in Birmingham, becoming cook in a large Jewish household on the Hagley Road. It was in Birmingham that she met my grandfather, Joseph Rogers, nine years her senior, but born in Pengam and a skilled worker in the metal industries. They married in Birmingham, which was where my mother was born in 1938. The very real threat posed by Luftwaffe raids drove the family back to Monmouthshire in about 1940, but after my grandfather's early death aged just forty-six in 1947 my grandmother returned to work, this time as cook in the local school in Pontnewydd.

I can imagine that my grandmother would have enjoyed reading this book. She would have recognised the descriptions of the drudgeries of domestic labour, of the status hierarchies of which employer and employee were so conscious, and of the homesickness and unhappiness sometimes occasioned by having to seek employment far from home. Of course there were worse jobs, and much worse lives to lead, but few of us can regret that the clearly demarcated world of master and servant has now largely passed away. For young women in contemporary society the opportunities are much greater in education and in the world of work (even if gender equality remains an elusive prize), and social mobility is a reality to a degree largely unimaginable in the Wales of Mary Thomas or even that of Nancy Rogers.

Rosemary Scadden, whom I am proud to note once worked with me on the M.Sc.Econ. (Women's Studies) at Cardiff University in the 1990s, has in this volume captured the essence of the experience of Welsh domestic servants in the first half of the twentieth century. Through painstaking oral history research she has interwoven the vivid memories of many Welsh women to tell a story that, remarkably, has never been adequately assessed. Through personal testimonies, by means of their own words, we are granted an insight into what was a very common phase in the lives of generations and a shared reference point in our culture. I hope that those who read this important book will raise their own questions with their own families in order to understand better the contours and limitations of the world we have lost.

Chris Williams, Cardiff University

Introduction

We all, men and women alike, have some knowledge of domesticity, of cooking, cleaning and laundry. Most of us spend as little time as possible on these boring, repetitive, irksome and often solitary chores; indeed, we now have many labour-saving devices that do the work for us, releasing us to follow more enjoyable and often more remunerative occupations. It should not therefore be too difficult to put ourselves in the place of the women whose testimony underpins the pages of this book. However what is more difficult is imagining what it was like, at the age of fourteen, to work more than twelve hours a day for strangers, far away from home.

Although this book looks in detail at the lives of Welsh girls who went into service between the two World Wars, the same conditions applied to working-class girls throughout Britain and probably many other parts of the world too. Thousands of girls had no choice but to take very low paid, arduous jobs as maids, and instead of spending happy times during their formative adolescence, they became drudges, with no opportunity to fulfil their potential.

The Second World War, of course marks a huge watershed in history. But when considering the social, gender and technological history of Britain, one can't help wondering whether the 1940s would have proved a significant milestone anyway. As a result of the general availability of electricity, all manner of machines and gadgets were developed that removed the necessity of servants in most households. Families became smaller and women were able to see beyond the interminable housework of their forebears. Domestic service was once the largest employer of women and young girls.

In the course of my professional life as a television researcher, I met a number of elderly women who told me enough about their lives as young domestic servants to make me curious. An old lady in Merthyr told me a particularly harrowing tale of how she was taken to London at the age of fourteen by friends of her widowed stepmother to help in a convalescent home in Kensington. On her days off she would sit in Kensington Gardens until the clock struck six and then go home to bed as she had no money and had nothing else to do. She found another job in the East End of London where the couple for whom she worked would lock her out of the house when they went out. She was a tiny little lady, and had to stand on a box in order to reach the wash tub in the yard, when doing the washing in all weathers.

On signing up to do a master's degree in Women Studies at Cardiff University, I had no problem in deciding what the subject matter of my dissertation should be when the time came. I would find a number of former domestic servants and record their testimony, women whose working lives corresponded neatly to the period between the two wars when, coincidentally, the practice of sending young girls from Wales into service virtually ceased. It was a timely study, capturing the memories of these women just before it was too late.

I advertised in a free paper especially targeted at the retired and I was inundated with replies. I had asked for women to get in touch if they had been in service and now lived within a twenty-five mile radius of Cardiff, where I lived; I intended to visit them and record the interviews. I had replies from as far afield as Aberdeen, Gosport, Bristol, Yorkshire and the Midlands. I had obviously struck a chord when I called them 'a lost generation' in my appeal. Very often their first words to me on the telephone were, 'You were right, we didn't have a chance!' For my academic study, I had only really needed six respondents, but such was their enthusiasm I went to see eighteen women, as well as accepting a tape and a long letter from two others respectively. I have since collected other testimonies as and when I have had the opportunity.

Almost two decades have passed since I conducted this study, and it now forms the basis for a lecture. Such has been the interest when I speak to different groups that I decided that a book would be the next step. There are plenty of written histories of such notable women as Florence Nightingale, Christabel Pankhurst or Marie Stopes, but not many documenting experiences of the less glorious.

There are even fewer books that describe the trials and tribulations of the mass of women. Even if some of us like to romanticize and imagine that our forbears were of noble birth, rich heiresses or even successful courtesans, most of them fall into the humble category of general servant or 'ag lab', as I once heard agricultural labourers described when I was a guest speaker at a family history group. Historians appear to have taken servants for granted, in the same way that their employers expected them always to be unobtrusive.

Tracing my own family directly through the female line, I found that my great grandmother's mother was one such servant girl. Maria Harding, born in 1824 on the Badminton estate, met her husband Robert Lloyd in London, where they were both living as servants in Carnaby Street. They married in St Martin-in-the-Fields in 1848. Her daughter, also Maria, became a cook in Newport.

After giving my talk, instead of inviting the usual questions, I turn the tables and ask for stories from the floor. I have heard many new tales in this way. I have been told also, however, of a mother or aunty or sister who had been in service but who was now deceased and whose stories would remain unheard. Those whose elderly relatives are still alive, I urge to rush home and record their memories immediately to pass on to future generations. When we are older, the long-term memory is often more reliable than the short-term one, and the recall of vivid and precise details of a way of life long gone will always engage our imagination and wonder.

Some of the women gave me the impression that they were permanently scarred by their time in service. Many recalled how they felt on the day they left home, the home sickness, the fear of making mistakes and of going out and about in London. On the other hand, others spoke of the pleasure of having plenty to eat for the first time, the joy of being surrounded by beautiful things and the satisfaction of performing their duties well.

Welsh girls, who entered domestic service in the 1920s and 1930s were shackled by poverty and became a 'lost generation'. Although many qualified for the grammar school by passing the entrance examination, they were, unlike many of their brothers, unable to benefit from such an education as their families could not afford to support them there. Thousands of girls had no choice but to take very low paid, arduous jobs as domestics servicing the more well-to-do, usually a long way from home.

I recorded the interviews I conducted with the women who volunteered to help me in my study, giving them an opportunity to speak for themselves. In the following chapters we shall learn why they were forced to leave home and how, in their own words, they faced those testing times.

Chapter 1

An Overview of Domestic Service

T HE REASONS FOR keeping a servant may seem obvious but there are other conditions besides those of general usefulness and practicality, because the servant was often the outward sign of distinction, in addition to being a source of labour. Generally speaking there were two groups of servants – indoor and outdoor. It was the men usually who worked outside, as gardeners, grooms or handymen and later chauffeurs. The now famous 'Lost Gardens of Heligan' in Cornwall, and many others like them, declined when all the gardeners left, never to return, after 1914. The Duke of Westminster had thirty-five outdoor gardeners alone and another seventeen for the glasshouses. But he also had fifty indoor servants. Indeed, a ratio of three or four servants to each member of the family was quite common in the wealthiest of homes. In large establishments there were male footmen, boot boys, a personal manservant and, of course, the most important of all servants, the butler. Women, on the other hand, worked indoors, as cooks, laundresses and maids.

Up until 1777 there were more indoor male servants than female ones, but in a move to finance the American War of Independence and simultaneously to release men to join the Navy to fight that war, a tax was levied on male indoor servants. This tax was not repealed until 1937, by which time service had become a predominantly female occupation. Consequently, the employment of male indoor staff would lend a greater cachet to both the establishment and the employee.

Before examining the role of the female servants it is worth looking briefly at the male house staff. The derivation of the word 'butler' reminds us what, originally, his main role was. It is a corruption of the French word '*bouteillier*', meaning 'cupbearer', and his real duty lay in keeping a good cellar. Wine came in casks and was bottled at home, by the butler. It was his job to serve it and all the things associated with it – the glassware, the spirits, the cigars etc., and in his Butler's Pantry, he would store, prepare and clean his accoutrements.

As well as running errands, a footman would do all the really dirty jobs early in the morning – cleaning the boots and shoes, the knives, the silver, the lamps. He would also help serve the food in his spotless white cotton gloves (good for holding hot dishes and disguising his grime-ingrained hands). He would wear work clothes for the dirty work and a special livery for any time he was to be seen in public. He might even have been chosen more for his height, and the shape and the turn of his calf, rather than for his domestic skills.

Unless the household was very large and grand, when there would have been a male steward at its head, a butler second in command, the chief female servant would have been the housekeeper. Mrs Beeton recommends that

> She should have a head for accounts and that her honesty and sobriety must be beyond reproach.

The housekeeper would represent the mistress of the house below stairs, and would be expected to have all her mistress's fine qualities, serving her household as if she were serving her own family. Indeed by the time she had reached this lofty position her employers would have been like her own family, her long years in service often meaning that she would have probably lost touch with her own kin. Not only would she need to be a good organiser but she would have built up a great practical knowledge over the

No. 333—2.

INLAND REVENUE.

LICENCE.—FOR ONE MALE SERVANT £0 15s. 0d.
32 & 33 Vict., cap. 14.

No. _2_ _Taff Well_ Collection.

Cardiff Div. or Ride.

William Evans

of _Pany_ _garn_ in the Parish

of _Caiysch_ in the County of _Glam_

is hereby authorized to employ ONE MALE SERVANT from the day of the date hereof until the 31st day of December next following; he having paid the sum of FIFTEEN SHILLINGS for this Licence.

Dated at _Taff Well_ this _10_

day of _Jany_ 187_6_.

Granted by _Mudyad Umma_

NOTICE.

If a MALE SERVANT be kept after the 31st December in any year, a fresh Declaration must be filled up and delivered, and a new Licence obtained before the expiration of the month of January following.

Licence to serve   (Don Llewellyn)

years. She would have her own sitting room, which would in effect be her office. Nearby would be the still room where she would manufacture ales, wines, cordials, scents and some medicines. In a very big establishment she would even have her own maid, who would clean the still room and keep the housekeeper's fire going.

Next in line was the cook, and her relationship with her domestic superior could often be fraught, as each sought to get one over the other. However, the housekeeper was responsible for ordering the supplies and would even take over some aspects of the cooking, particularly food preservation, making jams and pickles in season.

The cook might have resented the fact that the housekeeper could come in and out of her kitchen as and when she liked, might have liked to deal with the tradesmen herself so that she could pocket the occasional backhander. That is not to say that some women would have worked together in perfect harmony!

The cook would have to get up early to set the dough for breakfast, but the one who had to get up the earliest would be the scullery maid. She would have to light the fire in the kitchen ready for cook and boil water for the family to wash, when they rose. The scullery maid also had to clean and prepare the vegetables and the meat – skin rabbits, pluck poultry etc. Open fires meant that the cooking pots became blackened from the soot, making them very difficult for this poor wretch to scour clean, inside and out, with vinegar and coarse sand. Some households also had a kitchen maid whose position was somewhere between the two. This kitchen maid would also be responsible for cooking sauces and gravies, as well as taking a share of the laborious tasks described above, her ambition would be to become a cook herself one day. The number of women in a kitchen would, of course, depend on the size of the establishment and the family they served.

The laundry would be done away from the kitchen and in a large establishment there would be staff dedicated solely to this task. The soiled linen was soaked for a day, every Monday, and only actually washed on the Tuesday. Even in quite small households, the larger items were very often put out to be done elsewhere. When I was a child, I remember the commercial laundry man coming to our very modest semi to collect the dirty sheets and return the clean ones. The large brown paper parcel always looked so enticing and I would love to check the returned items from the laundry book. Not only was washing arduous, there remained the problem of what do with acres of wet sheets, in small houses where usually only one fire was burning and that in the living room. The British climate, after all, is just not conducive to the easy drying of clothes outdoors.

Ironing was the next chore. The word 'iron' has, of course, become so totally absorbed into our language that we forget that originally it was literally a lump of iron that had been fashioned in the local foundry. Irons were made of different weights and numbered accordingly. Several women have told me that a no.7 was known as a 'goose' and a no.10 was a heavy one used by a tailor. Most homes used a no.3. Two irons would be put on the stove to heat up; one was kept on the hob whilst the other was in use. There was a real skill in ironing, knowing when it was hot enough and when not too hot. Whenever I ask a group of women how to test a hot iron they all shout in unison, 'Spit on it!' Not so many know how to test a cooler iron. I remember seeing women holding irons very close to their cheeks to gauge its temperature. Early electric irons were very temperamental and the power source was the electric light socket, which meant standing on a chair to make the contact. Although most of us use an ironing board today, they were not universal before the Second World War, so women often talk of ironing on the table with a special blanket placed over it to protect the wood. But, however it was done, it was a hot and demanding job.

Housemaids were used for cleaning the areas beyond the kitchen. Carpets were cleaned by sweeping them with either moist tea leaves or with freshly pulled grass, both substances leaving a pleasant aroma which would refresh a room. In the afternoon the housemaid would then change from her working clothes into a black dress with a small white apron, and perform lighter duties, such as answering the front door bell and serving afternoon tea.

Some establishment ran to upper and under housemaids, but there were no hierarchical distractions in these titles, merely a pointer as to which part of the room they worked. The under maid would clean everything below the dado rail, including the carpets and the fires; the upper maid would clean everything on the surfaces and above. This clear demarcation of duties was a practical way of cleaning a very large room that may have contained many precious ornaments and pictures. The housekeeper could easily check how diligent each maid had been.

It was the chambermaid who carried the breakfast tray into the bedroom, which then became her main area of responsibility. Her most irksome task would be to empty the slops each morning and scour the chamber pots. Hot water had to be carried upstairs from the kitchen and then back down again to be disposed of after use. The bedrooms were often a long way from the kitchen and running up and down the stairs all the time, carrying heavy loads, would have been exhausting work. The kitchen was deliberately placed away from the living quarters of the family, wherever possible, in order to prevent fire spreading to the main living area. In addition any cooking smells would be less likely to permeate the house and the noise of the servants would be kept to a minimum.

To keep the beds comfortable, the mattresses had to be turned daily in order to spread the feathers more evenly as they tended to clump together and would then feel lumpy. They were often arranged like the ones in the fairy story of the princess and the pea, with a number of them piled one on top of another. At the bottom would be the straw palliasse; at the top, the best feather mattress usually a new one every year.

Finally, there were the personal servants – the valet and the waiting or lady's maid. It was the valet's duty to tend to all his master's creature comforts – shaving, hairdressing, running messages and caring for his clothes. He would always help to dress and undress him, often selecting the correct clothes for a particular occasion. The better off had clothes for every occasion, whether they were hunting, fishing, shooting, dining, or smoking.

The lady's maid was similarly employed, but she also had to be capable of dressing her mistress's hair. Here Mrs Beeton emphasises that this is the most important skill and even advises the maid to take lessons. She also suggests that the maid should take an interest in fashion by reading magazines. In this way she would have ideas of how to alter clothes, for the lady's maid had to have the talents of a milliner and seamstress at her fingertips. In addition, mending and spot cleaning the clothes had to be done – grease spots, wax and ink occasionally had to be removed. Mrs B includes a number of handy hints and recipes. To clean silk or ribbons she suggests the following:

½ pint gin: ½lb honey: ½lb soft soap: ½ pint water. Mix well and scrub into soiled site. Rinse in 3 rinses of clean cold water.

We should remember too the very personal nature of a lady's maid's duties such as 'lacing her mistress's stays and adjusting her linen smoothly'. Very often she would be party to the most intimate of secrets, possibly whether the master was currently sleeping with his wife or not; indeed she would hear all the family gossip. One of the most important qualities of a lady's maid, therefore, would be discretion. Ironing was another skill that was of more practical value, especially in the summer when the delicate muslin dresses, with all their frills and flounces would need special attention. Should the mistress have jewellery, it was also the maid who was expected to clean and care for it.

One other domestic group remains – a very special class all on their own, and they were the nursery staff who cared for the children. These women often found themselves in a very awkward social position: they felt superior to the house staff, but could not become too familiar with the family, their employers. Very often they saw more of the children than the parents did and a lasting bond was frequently developed between them. There were cases of nursery staff serving three generations of one family.

Indoor work was as seasonal as outdoor work. In winter only the day-to-day housework could be accomplished because so much heavy labour was required to keep the fires, downstairs and upstairs. Spring-cleaning is a dwindling ritual today, but the original reason for having such an all-out effort was to remove the dust and dirt that had accumulated because of the winter coal fires. The house had to put on a bright appearance, and be, to quote Mrs B, 'in unison with the season'. The fine weather provided an opportunity to take carpets outside for a beating, to wash blankets and dry them outside, to change and wash the curtains.

Summer was the time for mending and repairing household items, preserving fruit, making jam and pickling vegetables. Food preservation was continued into autumn when stores were laid up for the winter and the house and clothes prepared for the cold weather. Most of December was spent in preparing for Christmas. We should remember that food was seasonal and life had a rhythm connected with nature.

Here is a contemporaneous observation of domestic service, found in *Goodbye To All That* by Robert Graves (1929)

> My mother and father were never of the aggressive, shoot-'em down type. They were Liberals, or more strictly Liberal-Unionist. In religious theory, at least, they treated their employees as fellow-creatures. But social distinctions remained clearly defined, that was religion too:
>
> > He made them highly or lowly,
> > And ordered their estates.
>
> I can well recall the tone of my mother's voice when she informed the maids that they could have what was left of the pudding, or scolded the cook for some carelessness. It was a forced hardness, made almost harsh by embarrassment. My mother was gentle by nature. She would, I believe, have given a lot to be able to dispense with servants altogether. They were a foreign body in the house. I remember what the servants' bedrooms used to look like. By a convention of the times they were the only rooms in the house that had no carpet or linoleum; they were on the top landing on the dullest side of the house. The gaunt, unfriendly-looking beds and the hanging-cupboards with faded cotton curtains, instead of wardrobes with glass doors as in the other rooms. All this uncouthness made me think of the servants as somehow not quite human. The type of servant that came was not very good; only those with not particularly good references would apply for a situation where there were ten in the family. And because it was such a large house, and there was hardly a single tidy person in the household, they were constantly giving notice. There was too much work, they said. To that the tendency to think of them as only half human was increased; they never had time to get fixed as human beings.

Although it is an obvious question we must ask why did people such as these, keep servants then? The quick answer is that we all prefer someone else to do the dirty work for us! However, we must understand that there was a real need for staff and not just for the landed gentry. It was the sheer inefficiency of the heating and cooking facilities in many houses, that contributed to the constant demand for domestic labour.

Open fires provide both warmth and heat for cooking. Until gas and then electricity were piped into our houses, open fires had to be maintained. They are greedy, needy beasts requiring constant attention, stoking, poking and feeding. They also create dirt and grime, not just inside the home but in the surrounding environment too, which adds to the work – the washing of clothes and all that that entails. We sometimes use the word 'charwoman' to describe a daily help, a part-time cleaner. The word is actually associated with fire – 'char – to burn, to scorch' – the woman who cleared up the ashes.

Conditions barely changed for staff, whether they were working in the 1730s, the 1830s or the 1930s. So long as there was a supply of cheap labour, innovation by the way of developing labour-saving devices was discouraged. If you can pay women cheaply to boil, mangle and hang the washing out to dry, then the development of an all-singing, all-dancing washing machine that works even when you are not there will take longer to invent! As long as it is not your knees that are taking the pounding from scrubbing and your hands that are red raw from washing dishes in soda, then you will be happy to pay someone else to do it.

> The general servant, or maid of all work, is perhaps the only one of her class deserving of commiseration.

So said Mrs Beeton in her famous book of household management in 1859. She then takes forty-five pages to describe the duties of the various female domestic servants, duties that were also carried out by the women I interviewed, some seventy years later. Conditions had barely changed in 200 years.

The classic television series *Upstairs, Downstairs* broadcast in the early 1970s and recently revived, has left a lasting, if somewhat romantic notion of what service entailed. The 2001 feature film *Gosford Park* is in a similar vein with as much intrigue below stairs as there is action above. These are not however typical images of a servant's life, either in Victorian times or the inter-war years, especially so because the vast majority of servants worked alone.

On the eve of World War One, the Women's Industrial Council carried out a survey of domestic servants, inviting both the mistresses and servants to take part. Predictably, many of the mistresses complained about the quality of servants, and the servants about their poor conditions. The main area of contention, for both parties, was the generally held view that there was a social stigma attached to service.

The reason why the Victorian attitude of employing a resident maid continued to prevail right up to the outbreak of the Second World War was that it was the mark of respectability. Indeed the new middle classes created a fresh demand for servants for that reason. Wives were expected to be idle as that increased the status of the family and was linked to the domestic ideal. They were seen as a symbol and reward for that reason. In the inter-war period, what the better-off saw as the 'servant problem', a shortage, was due more to the excessive demand for labour. Because of the meagre wages paid to staff, even large numbers of lower middle-class families could afford to employ one maid.

Therefore despite the gradual expansion of industrial, clerical and retail employment for young women after the First World War, the largest occupation for this group remained domestic service right into the 1930s. This actually increased slightly between 1921 and 1931, when it accounted for 24.3 per cent of the young female workforce.[1]

In his autobiography *All Done From Memory* Osbert Lancaster writes rather poignantly,

> How different it all was in the years before 1914! Then the stucco, creamy bright, gleamed softly beneath what seems in reminiscence to have been a perpetually cloudless sky. Geraniums in urns flanked each brass-enriched front door,

---

[1] *Census of England and Wales, 1921*, Occupation Tables, 1924, table 3; *Census of England and Wales, 1931*, Occupation Tables, 1934, table 3.

while over the area railings moustachioed policemen made love to buxom cooks. And in every street there hung, all summer long, the heavy scent of limes.

The angel who drove the original inhabitants out of this gilt-edged Eden, not with a flaming sword but by a simple vanishing trick, was the domestic servant. The houses, even the small ones like ours, were planned on generous lines and labour-saving was still not only an unrealised but un-thought-of ideal. Fortunately my parents, whose joint income at the time of my birth amounted to all of £600 a year, were able to maintain a cook, a housemaid, a nurse and a boot-boy; my mother, moreover, had been through the hard school of a Victorian grandmother's household, and herself undertook such specialised, and now obsolete, labours as cleaning the chandeliers, washing the rubber-plant and superintending the linen.

Chapter 2

Conditions in South Wales
in the Inter-War Years

T HE LOT OF the Welsh domestic servant cannot be divorced from the prevaling economic situation of the period. Why, after all, did these girls go into service? Could it be, as some historians contend, that the Depression played the same role in Welsh history as the famine did in Irish history?[2]

Since the end of the eighteenth century, the happy juxtaposition of iron ore, limestone and coal made the valleys of South Wales one of the main centres of heavy industries in Britain. From a quiet, sparsely populated, farming region, its increase in population was nothing short of explosive, with immigrants being attracted to the 'black Klondyke' from the rest of Wales, the Midlands, Scotland and a substantial number from famine-racked Ireland. The coast, also conveniently to hand, with the ports of Cardiff, Newport, Barry and Swansea, grew equally in prosperity.

The great economic depression that followed the First World War was worldwide. Millions were unemployed in the United States, in Europe and in the other heavily industrialised parts of Britain, namely Tyneside and Central Scotland, as well as South Wales. The country was divided roughly into two parts,

---

[2] Chris Williams, *Democratic Rhondda; Politics & Society 1885–1951* PhD Thesis. University of Wales 1991

UNEMPLOYMENT
IN
MERTHYR TYDFIL

A Survey made at the request
of the Merthyr Settlement

by

Gwynne Meara, M.A.

Price 6d.

The Proceeds from the Sale of this Pamphlet
will be used to further the work of the
Settlement among the Unemployed
in Merthyr Tydfil.

NEWTOWN:
The Montgomeryshire Printing Company, Ltd.

From the next table it will be seen that it is, in the main, much easier to place girls outside the district than boys, largely because of the opening for girls as domestic servants. In Merthyr there is a Home Training Centre which is doing good work in fitting girls for domestic service; (during the year 1933 103 juveniles completed a course of training at the Centre, 97 of whom were placed as servants).

Year ended.	Boys.			Girls.			Total.
	Number placed locally.	Number placed elsewhere.	Total Number placed.	Number placed locally.	Number placed elsewhere.	Total Number placed.	
Nov. 1st, 1924 to 31.7.25.			68			20	88
31.7.26			56			10	66
31.7.27			56			24	80
31.7.28	91	8	99	26	5	31	130
31.7.29	76	66	142	20	4	24	166
31.7.30	90	33	123	13	25	38	161
31.7.31	62	23	85	26	42	68	153
31.7.32	104	10	114	19	47	66	180
31.7.33	136	14	150	66	91	157	307

That the Juvenile Employment Bureau might be used more by School leavers is obvious from the following table, showing the number of juveniles leaving the elementary schools of the district who utilised the services of the Bureau and its officer, and the number of school leavers who utilised the facilities afforded by the Bureau who were placed in employment :—

Year ended.	No. of Juveniles eligible by age to leave School.		No. of School leavers who utilise the Bureau.				No. of School leavers utilising Bureau who were placed in employment.			
	Boys.	Girls	Boys	%	Girls	%	Boys	%	Girls	
31.7.25(a)	419	379	111	26.4	53	13.9	11	9.9	1	1.8
31.7.26	620	606	117	18.9	58	9.6	9	7.7	1	1.7
31.7.27	657	605	128	19.5	58	9.6	11	8.6	3	5.2
31.7.28	572	586	119	20.8	54	9.2	16	13.4	2	3.7
31.7.29	598	602	147	24.6	49	8.1	12	8.2	2	4.1
31.7.30	572	537	111	19.4	45	8.4	22	19.8	3	6.7
31.7.31(b)	416	444	85	20.4	38	8.5	18	21.2	2	5.3
31.7.32	394	424	97	24.6	65	15.3	19	19.5	7	10.7
31.7.33	464	427	191	41.1	99	23.1	33	17.2	20	20.2

Boys and girls from the secondary schools are using the Bureau much more than formerly, and the Bureau is increasingly useful to them in placing them in employment when they have left school, as the following table shows :—

Year ended.	Secondary School Pupils.			
	No. Registered at the Bureau.		No. placed in Employment	
	Boys.	Girls.	Boys.	Girls.
31.7.30	42	14	11	4
31.7.31	31	10	7	3
31.7.32	97	65	19	7
31.7.33	58	38	17	10

Opportunities for girls: a page from *Unemployment in Merthyr Tydfil* (1933).

the depressed areas of Wales and the North, with regions of comparative affluence in the Midlands, the South and the East. Britain was no longer the workshop of the world, and the dole queues were overwhelmingly peopled by miners, cotton workers, shipbuilders and metal-workers.

In 1936 the South Wales Coalfield was designated by the Labour Party as one of the four designated distressed areas of Great Britain. Coal mining had accounted for more than 50% of all the 'insured workers' in 1923 but this had dropped to 37% by 1935. The rate of unemployment was four times that of London and it was the number of long term unemployed that was particularly high. It was noted that nearly 300,000 men, women and children had officially migrated from the area over a period of fourteen years and this was out of a population of one-and-three-quarter million.

> Unemployment, up to the end of 1920, was negligible, but as conditions in the (Coal) Industry became more and more unsatisfactory from 1921 onwards, signs of the depression became more obvious, until by April 1927, the situation was indeed serious.[3]

A report by the Labour Party in 1937 ends with a very dramatic paragraph:

> Only the most drastic action by the state can save the people of South Wales from the suffering and misery and despair which for long years has engulfed them.[4]

It was the prolonged nature of the unemployment in South Wales which made it more severe than in any other part of Britain, indeed its unprecedented duration had such a devastating effect. The region's over-specialisation in its narrow range of heavy industries – iron, steel and coal – made it especially vulnerable to the Slump. The decrease in the demand for coal was dramatic as industry and

---

[3] *Unemployment in Merthyr Tydfil: A Survey made at the request of the Merthyr Settlement* (1933), page 6
[4] *South Wales: Report of the Labour Party's Commission of Enquiry into the Distressed Areas (May 1937), Page 130*

shipping converted from steam to oil. Coal from South Wales had kept the Royal Navy afloat, as it had the formerly very active British merchant fleet. In addition France was one of the major markets for Welsh coal. However by the terms of the Treaty of Versailles in 1921, the rich coal mines of the Saar district of Germany were to pass to France as part reparation for the damage caused by the 1914-18 War. Not only did earnings fall, but the number of men employed in the industry fell over the period from 257,613 in 1919 to 128,774 in 1939. There was a ripple effect throughout the whole economy as with reduced purchasing power, local shops and services also suffered. Some small businesses could not survive as the Depression spread like a relentless cancer:

> The South Wales Miners' Federation emphasized the social significance of the tremendous fall in the total wages paid, from £30,500,000 in 1934 to about £14,000,000 in 1936.[5]

In addition to the general worldwide slump three quarters of a million women had been dismissed from factories and workshops, rail and bus companies in 1919, to make way for the returning ex-service men. This huge pool of unemployed women could not possible be absorbed by the limited alternative occupations open to them. Training in domestic service for working-class girls was seen as the sensible solution. Most of the posts subsequently obtained were in private houses or institutions, with board and lodgings provided. Not only would it provide them with much needed work, but living away from home would alleviate the strain on the over-stretched family resources and they could even contribute some of their income back to Wales. Men, on the other hand, were often housed in work camps, adding to the cost of these schemes.

Many male workers were encouraged to migrate to more prosperous areas in England, like Cowley, near Oxford, to make cars; Slough, to make chocolate; High Wycombe, to make furniture; the coalfields of Kent, or the lighter metal industries of Birmingham. The emigration figures to the USA, Canada,

---

[5] *South Wales: Report of the Labour Party's Commission of Enquiry into the Distressed Areas (May 1937), Page 18*

Australia, New Zealand and South Africa soared during this time. The Press frequently wrote articles to encourage emigration to the 'Dominions'. The *Free Press of Monmouthshire* carried such an article in September 1927 –

> At present the Dominions call for domestic workers, and so far as women and girls are concerned, Government aid, in the form of assisted passages and assured employment, is practically restricted to these. The reason is clear. Neither the British nor Dominion Governments can take responsibility of encouraging and assisting women to leave their homes in this country for the Dominions unless employment at the other end of the journey is certain. In all the Dominions, with the exception of South Africa, household workers are needed in large numbers. . . . Unhappily, also, housework is the Cinderella of women's callings, and it is unlikely that that which is shunned here will make a very strong appeal across the ocean, especially to women who have tested and have confidence in their ability to do other things. The result is that the call goes unheeded by just those women suited to a life in the Dominions and of whom the Dominions have most need. For it must be borne in mind that the women who go overseas are not only workers in particular callings: they are potential wives and mothers. Common sense demands, therefore, that they should be representative of the best qualities of our race. To say this is not in any way to disparage the houseworker. On the contrary, a practical knowledge of all branches of domestic economy should be possessed by every woman who aspires to a home of her own. What needs to be done is to raise the status of domestic employment by improvement in wages and conditions so that it will be regarded no longer as a distasteful form of drudgery, but as an occupation worthy of any woman who wishes to earn her own living. In the Dominions a good deal has been done in that direction

There were advertisements too for young girls to seek their fortune as domestics in these far-flung countries. Also in 1927, the Salvation Army took the idea of sending the unemployed to Australia a step further by chartering a ship of the White Star Line called *The Vedic* and put out a press release stating:

> Young women, experienced and inexperienced, willing to undertake household duties, are in much demand in Australia, and for those who place themselves under their care the Army guarantees situations at good wages. The living conditions in Australia are stated to be extremely comfortable. Free passages will be given to approved experienced domestics, while suitable domesticated women, inexperienced, but willing to do housework, will be granted nominated passages for which the rate is £16. 10s, which will be repayable by monthly instalments out of wages. This money, however, will be returned to the young women at the end of twelve months provided they have completed a year's domestic service satisfactorily.

In 1928 the Ministry of Labour inaugurated a transference programme from the depressed areas to the more prosperous ones. In the six years from 1927 to 1933 almost 20,000 male juveniles under the age of eighteen were transferred and almost the same numbers were again transferred between 1934 and 1936. Indeed,

> The only hope for the school leaving population seems to be in areas outside the Borough. The prospect before boys and girls leaving school each year in Merthyr are gloomy indeed.[6]

It was believed that men who did not have years of work experience behind them, missed work less; they would adapt to unemployment more easily. They had not got the habit of work. It was for them that occupational centres and training schemes were most needed, keeping them physically and mentally fit for work, when work eventually came. Or, as it turned out, when war came.

Conditions were less severe in the coastal towns of South Wales where there was a rising professional middle class. Some people were enjoying a richer life with longer holidays, shorter hours and

---

[6] *Unemployment in Merthyr Tydfil: A Survey made at the request of the Merthyr Settlement* (1933), page 10

Local Unemployment

THE incidence of unemployment is seen in the following table, which gives the numbers of insured persons, and the percentages unemployed on March 15, 1937, in the employment exchange areas of the South Wales Industrial Region :

	Insured Persons	Percentage Unemployed
Eastern Valley of Monmouthshire		
Blaenavon	3,460	28.0
Pontypool	13,510	25.5
Pontnewydd	2,740	35.1
Western Valleys of Monmouthshire		
Brynmawr	2,610	56.7
Blaina	2,720	43.6
Abertillery	6,930	27.7
Ebbw Vale	9,780	14.7
Tredegar	7,210	22.0
Blackwood	5,260	24.2
Newbridge	8,460	12.6
Risca	4,960	25.7
Rhymney Valley		
Pontlottyn	2,660	43.3
Bargoed	15,410	20.3
Caerphilly	9,320	29.0
Merthyr Vale		
Merthyr Tydfil	19,940	45.6
Aberdare Valley		
Aberdare	12,790	30.0
Mountain Ash	9,160	24.5
Rhondda Valleys		
Ferndale	5,990	55.9
Porth	8,410	32.5
Pontypridd	12,110	40.1
Treorchy	15,530	24.3
Tonypandy	10,550	41.4
Tonyrefail	4,560	25.3
Newport-Cardiff District		
Newport	28,430	20.4
Cardiff	69,940	20.1
Barry	8,930	32.0
Taffs Well	1,840	21.7
Port Talbot-Bridgend-Pontyclun District		
Pontyclun	2,630	18.4
Cymmer	3,640	13.3
Maesteg	6,400	34.6
Pontycymmer	2,620	30.3
Ogmore Vale	3,100	21.5
Aberkenfig	2,410	26.9
Bridgend	4,090	24.4
Port Talbot	13,450	23.0
Vale of Neath and Dulais Valley		
Resolven	6,920	5.2
Neath	17,760	18.1

4

Grim reading from *South Wales: Report of the Labour Party's Commission of Enquiry into the Distressed Areas (May 1937)*

higher wages. They had motor cars, cinemas, radio sets, electrical appliances and pleasant housing.

In stark contrast, twenty miles north of Cardiff many inhabitants of the Rhondda Valleys were dependent on soup kitchens in order to survive.

This widespread deprivation went on for years as the following documentary evidence indicates. Statistics show that in 1937 out of a population of 200,000 there were over 16,000 unemployed miners.

> In the seven weeks ending November 14 1936, a weekly average of 14,616 persons received poor relief. As a result of a 1936 malnutrition survey of 21,845 elementary school children, 5,927 or 27.1 per cent, were certified as requiring additional nourishment. The corresponding percentage in 1935 was 14.6. Half the school children have inadequate shoes and clothing. There is widespread poverty.[7]

Ten years earlier there was a small piece in the *Glamorgan County Times* dated 22 February 1927 headed 'Relief for Miners' Dependents'. It goes on to say that:

> Over £11,000 has been dispensed in the East Glamorgan area in connection with the 'Lady Slesser Fund for the relief of miners' wives and children' . . . Of this nearly £1,600 was allocated to Rhondda West and £1,800 to Rhondda East. Altogether 4,500 cases were relieved, while in addition hundreds of sacks of clothing were given out. Furthermore, over 500 children were temporarily cared for in London homes during the stoppage.

In the very same paper there is a most comprehensive report on the Pontypridd Hospital Ball describing in great and fascinating detail the dresses of the one hundred or so ladies present, thus providing hard evidence of the polarity of life there. Miss Rowbotham, for example wore a 'peach coloured georgette dress, heavily sequined', but Mrs T D Davies was even more grandly attired wearing

---

[7] *South Wales: Report of the Labour Party's Commission of Enquiry into the Distressed Areas (May 1937), Page 12*

'Mushroom pink georgette and jade trimmed with fox fur'. It was not all doom and gloom, but the two sides of life were poles apart.

The ten thousand domestic servants from Wales who were working in London in 1934, and the thousands who remained in Wales working for the more prosperous, seemingly did join up the two sides of life. They left behind the poverty and bad housing, which for a substantial section of the South Wales population was a major feature in their lives, to watch, from the sidelines, the antics of the upper and middle classes.

George Thomas, Viscount Tonypandy, former Speaker of the House of Commons, wrote in his memoir:

> On my way to school every Monday morning during that great exodus I would see little family groups on the platform of Tonypandy railway station saying tearful farewells to somebody who had found work in Slough or Birmingham or Coventry or Nuneaton. In those days that was like going to China, because they did not know when they would be able to save enough to pay for a visit home.
>
> There was not a family in South Wales untouched by such misery: it was like a terrible war taking our people from us. My mother helped to clothe three hundred Valley girls who found jobs as domestic servants in English houses. Their clothes and railway fares were provided by the Distress Fund set up by the Lord Mayor of London, and deep bitterness filled us as one by one they left their homes. Far from being grateful, the cry on everybody's lips was: 'Our daughters are cheap skivvies for well-off people.'

Various government training establishments were set up throughout Britain, including one in Pontypridd called Jacobsdale where daughters of the unemployed were sent for eighteen weeks. They were trained in such skills as basic cookery, laundry, cleaning, bedmaking and the appropriate etiquette needed to be a parlour maid. The final week was residential to give the girls the experience of living away from home. At the end of their training, positions were found for the girls which they were obliged to take as their mothers had signed a paper before the training started to that effect. The advantage to the employer was that the new servant at least had had the corners knocked off, as it were:

> (It is) much easier to place girls outside the district than boys, largely because of the opening for girls as domestic servants. In Merthyr there is a Home Training Centre which is doing good work in fitting girls for domestic service; (during the year 1933 103 juveniles completed a course of training at the Centre, 97 of whom were placed as servants).[8]

Another such establishment, set up in 1932, was the Lapswood Domestic Training Centre housed in a mansion in Sydenham Hill, South London. Here six teachers trained forty girls over a period of three months. Their press release stated that

> the committee offers any British girl the chance of getting free of charge, a thorough training in up-to-date domestic science, three months' board and lodgings, and a good job and complete working outfit at the end of it. Since Lapswood opened six years ago, 1,287 perfect maids have been trained there.

---

[8] *Unemployment in Merthyr Tydfil: A Survey made at the request of the Merthyr Settlement* (1933), page 12

Chapter 3

Family Background

I T WAS QUITE remarkable that of the twenty women who replied to my appeal for former domestic servants to come forward, sixteen had been born in the mining valleys of South Wales. Of the two women born in England, one was also from a mining family and the other had returned to her extended family in Wales, when orphaned at the age of nine months. The remaining two contributors came from working-class families in Newport and Cardiff.

Many of their fathers worked, as one might have expected, in the mines in one capacity or another. Most were colliers; another was a haulier looking after the horses underground and one father was a stoker in the pit, stoking the boilers to make steam to enable the machinery above ground to work. A couple of fathers worked on the railway, which was considered to be a more secure occupation. Margaret C. lived in Cardiff and her father was a sailor, who was away from home for the most part; Nellie's father worked in an iron foundry. But what of Miriam?

> We were very poor. My father was a stonemason, a jadder, as they called it. He prepared the stone in Graig-y-resg, for the stonemason to dress the stone, piece working. If you had bad weather, you had no money – with all the family.

Hazel's father, on the other hand, was an invalid with a degenerative illness:

To be quite honest, I can't remember him working. I can remember him going on the big march to London. He collapsed when he got as far as Bridgend because he had an illness which we didn't know about then. He was taken to the cottage hospital in Bridgend. He went in when I was eight and he never came out.

Nancy was an exception. Although her father too was a miner, he was an overman (a managerial position) and they lived in the Midlands. She was better off than the other women I interviewed and only went into service as a precursor to a career in nursing. Her mother enrolled her as a maid in a nursing home to see if she could tolerate the medical environment:

It was an expensive business being a nurse then. We went for three months on probation and our parents had to buy the uniform for that three months, which cost a lot of money. There were three dresses, fourteen aprons, fourteen pairs of collars and fourteen sets of cuffs, black stockings and flat shoes, special shoes. All this had to be bought and at the end of the three months, if one wasn't suitable, that was an awful lot of money wasted. So my mother said to me, 'Right young lady. You want to be a nurse. We'll make sure that it's not going to be too much for you.'

Such was Phyllis's wonderful recall that one can almost hear her father speaking to her:

My father was a stoker in the no.9 pit in Tylorstown. My sister and I used to take his tea every Sunday. He'd have this cotton thing for a neck tie, a butcher's rag, they called it. There'd be huge fires, and he'd be shovelling in. We'd take a jack of tea and some lunch for him. We'd stay a little while and watch, then when we'd leave, he would come part of the way with us. Sweat would be pouring down his face, and he'd say, 'Now be careful! Mind the ropes.' Because the ropes were always on the go, if they did catch you they'd cut your leg off.

Floors & Furniture reflect the brilliance of
MANSION POLISH
which is equally good for Linoleum
In Tins 6d., 10½d. & 1/9. Large family tin 3/- contains 2 lbs. nett

The polishing at home would be nothing compared to the sheen expected when
these girls went into service. (Advertising Archives)

The size of their families ranged from just two to as many as thirteen siblings, and those women who came from the larger families were usually very familiar with domestic work, long before they did it for a living.

EUNICE
We were made as children to work as soon as we could toddle. We had to scrub the stairs and clean brass rods, all this sort of thing. We were made to do so.

CEINWEN
We all had to work in the house for our mother. We all had to do jobs, like washing the Welsh dresser with all the willow pattern. One had to do the pantry. One had to do the brass, which was all over the mantelpiece. We all had our jobs.

NELLIE
I was the fourth child. I had four brothers so I was the only girl. Unfortunately it meant that I had to help a lot in the house. I had to help with the washing. When I came home from school I had to lay the table for dinner and wash up before I went back to school, and do the same tea time. And on a Saturday, I had to polish the hall passage and scrub the flag stones out the front, from the front door to the kerb. I also had to clean windows, which I didn't like, so I made a poor job of it, so I got out of that. Why the boys didn't work I'll never know. They didn't help at all.

MARGARET D.
When I was a child, I was expected to work around the house; all the girls were expected, in those days, weren't they? It was training for you anyway. If you went to work or not, if you settled down and met someone, you'd know how to do things like cooking. I had good training at home, before I went away. I used to cook at an early age.

MEGAN

Our first job, I can remember when I went to school, was learning to wash up. My mother would say, 'Clear the table.' In turns we had to do it, and then we had to wash up in turns and wipe up. But I'll never forget it. When I was six I had promotion: I was allowed to scrub the window sills down and clean around the sink. That was great! And when I was about six-and-a-half, I was upgraded: I was allowed to scrub the toilet seat. It had to be white, believe you me. My mother always gave us some 'Kerol' disinfectant and we had to dip our brush in it and we had to wipe the handle of the toilet door and the chain. Then do it with a damp rag. When I think of some of the things my mother taught me! Then it came you had promotion when you were seven-and-a-half or eight: you had to scrub the pantry shelves.

PHYLLIS

We were always squabbling over the housework. My older sister, she had to do the big middle room; my other sister had to do the back kitchen with the flagstones – whiten the hearth, clean the fender, scrub the flagstones, then sprinkle sand over the back kitchen. Then in the middle room it was tiles and the rugs. We used to make the rugs between us, save all the old pieces of coloured rags, get a piece of sacking and sometimes there would be two or three of us with a peg and we'd make lovely coloured rugs. Imagine then, they had to be cleaned and shaken in the yard, before you could put them back.

I had to do the passage and all of a long flight of steps outside. I didn't like it at all. I wanted to do the middle kitchen, but I never had the chance.

ELIZABETH

I knew if I wanted three pence for the pictures, I had to do little jobs for it, cleaning the hen house or crushing the egg shells that went back into the chicken food. I had to take my baby sister with me when I was meeting my friends up the park. I often had to bathe and dress her, and before I left home, was doing some ironing for mother.

EILEEN

My mother was doing more sewing. I had to come home from school and clean and wash the dishes. I hated that sewing because I couldn't go out to play.

PHYLLIS

We weren't really old enough to do a lot. But my older sister did help a lot to look after us. She nursed some of the younger ones as they were still babies. As she was getting a bit older, she was going out and helping mothers that were having babies. So she was doing all the heavy work that is done on confinement. When she was out on those things, it would be done either by my other sister, or me.

MAY

I didn't have to help in the house, but my sister did. She was doing bread at the age of eight. She was the eldest daughter, so she knew what it was, after confinement and one thing and another. I feel sorry for my sister because she bore the brunt of everything. I remember her saying, one time, 'Oh Mam, not again!' But all this was done in our own language, Welsh. I think she must have had a sigh of relief when I was the last one.

There were exceptions; if they were the youngest in the family then they would not have been expected to help at home so when they did go away into service, the work came as a bit of a shock.

HILDA

My father worked underground I had six brothers; I was the only girl and the youngest. They all worked underground eventually. There was no alternative. My mother did not go out to work as she had enough to do, washing, ironing and cleaning. Being the last in the family, I was no use at all!

Most of the women appreciated how hard their mothers had to work; sharing the hardships often created a deep bond between them.

DOROTHY

I kiss her (photograph) every night . . . She had such a hard life and she never had a chance to have the ease I could have given her. She was a lovely mother, she was.

MARGARET C.

My mother used to do the best she could – buy haricot beans and a big pot of potatoes. They used to be a thing called 'gong soup'. She would boil this up with the potatoes and have some bacon bones. You would have those for nothing off the grocer in Bute Street and she'd boil those, boil the beans, put this soup in it. Anything to fill a hole and she would make a big suety pudding to fill the holes!

EUNICE

My mother used to write to me. My mother was sweet. She was a little doll, very small, proper little doll.

PHYLLIS

There were twelve children in the family: six boys and six girls. My mother was a very hard worker, a very hard worker. It was a big house, four bedrooms, big living room, kitchen, back yard. Well, she used to do all that.

She was very good with her meals. She was excellent baking her bread and her Christmas cake. I can still smell those Christmas cakes we used to fetch them from the bakehouse. She'd make about seven. When she made bread she again made about seven loaves. My brother and I would bring them up, and you know, the crusts would be hanging off these and we'd be dying to take them off, but she was a strict mother. She wasn't cruel in any way but very strict because with young boys and girls, growing up, she always had an eye on both sides, all the time.

She had the old tubs for washing and the scrubbing board. She would take in and do her own washing, which was a lot. It averaged about two-and-a-half hours between us all, so you can imagine. The cooking then was done at the old-fashioned fireplace, with the ovens by the side and hobs and brass rod and the big heavy kettle. Every Sunday she would make tart, but we always had good food, nothing fancy. She'd fill a huge iron saucepan, brimming to the top, with stews, dumplings and all that. And, in the morning a big saucepan full of porridge before school. Then we would come home teatime, she'd have something for us then – cake for our tea, salad or something like that. Supper time it was just a bit of bread and butter or a couple of biscuits before bed. We had to be in bed early. She didn't like us out late at all.

My mother was spotless, upstairs and downstairs. She had to go down a yard and up a very long garden to where the line was. She had the four bedrooms of bedding, all in the tub and on the rubbing board, and anything that had to be boiled, like the whites, were boiled in an iron boiler, on the fire in the back kitchen. All the whites were blued, to come out lovely and white then she'd take them up the garden where there was always the big line full. And we had nice weather; we seemed to have a lot of nice weather and this lovely line full of washing blowing. Funnily enough my father used to go up and bring it in. I can always see him coming back with a line full of washing.

MIRIAM
My mother spent all her time looking after her own mother and father and nine children. They used to send her around, when any of the family were not very well. She used to go around to do the washing, hard washing, with the old washing board. My mother was the drudge of the family.

Families looked after each other and, even though there were many children already to be looked after, Mary W was taken in by an aunt:

My mother died when I was nine months old. I was taken to Trehafod, Pontypridd, to stay with an aunt. After the funeral I was taken and stayed until she died when I was twenty-two. Her husband was working in the colliery and she had nine children and she brought me and her granddaughter up as well. We were both brought up together, two little orphans.

In the very large families, because of the wide age range of the siblings, the women very often did not know their brothers and sisters very well. The older children were already away working, or new babies appeared in the family whilst the women themselves were away in service. A lady I met after a lecture told me her father was the youngest of seventeen children. His elder sister went away to service and he never even met her until he was grown up and married with children of his own.

EUNICE

It was a shame really; you lost so much of your teen years, together.

CEINWEN

My Mam didn't work because she had too many children. She had twelve altogether when I was born, and there was another one born after I went away to work, a sister.

EUNICE

I had a sister seven years older who went into service at fourteen. She was sent up to London, but not to a big house. They had florist shops, but she had to see to the house and the cooking. Like all servants, she had to do everything.

DORIS

My sister, she had a sewing trade, with a dressmaker, which my mother paid for. You had to pay for everything then. After I went away, she wrote for a job as a sewing maid in another part of the country, Swansea way.

ANNIE

My mother had four children before the 1914–18 War and then she had five after the War. We were more or less two separate families. I had a sister, in with the four before the War, and she worked in a hospital in Bristol. The next sister, she was in domestic service and she went to London and ended up in Woking, Surrey. My next sister, she worked in Westgate Street, in Castle Court flats.

None of the mothers worked outside the home, in the way that women do today and so it was the father's income upon which the family depended. Even though they all came from financially poor homes, some were much poorer than others and their living conditions varied accordingly.

HAZEL

We lived in my grandfather's house. My grandparents came from Morriston. They were very poor down there, so they came up to Mountain Ash as mining jobs were quite well paid. My grandfather was a gaffer haulier, in charge of horses. He worked until he was a good age really. He had a little pension.

He was my mother's father, but he was like a father and everything to us too. He really brought us up. He was really Welsh speaking. My mother spoke Welsh, but father didn't so we were brought up as English, more or less, just picking up a bit of Welsh. We didn't speak Welsh in school, we were not allowed to. You spoke English. Down the mines they spoke Welsh, but when they got paid it was always in English. I shared a bed with my sister. My brother slept with my grandfather right until he was married. You just did it and that was it. There was often four in a bed.

DORIS

We didn't go to any soup kitchens or any thing like that, which a lot of children went to in those days. We had a dressmaker, who lived at the back of us; Miriam her name was. We always had our dresses made for us and I think she used to charge about half a crown to have a dress made.

NANCY

I was always aware that we were better off than most, but I think this was because my parents were very wise. My father always had a garden and an allotment. There was always plenty of food. We were never hungry: lots of other people were.

MARY K.

I was born in 1908 (13th January), one of twelve children, living in the Rhondda, in Treorchy. I was a miner's daughter and the housing conditions were shocking. Floods used to come in periodically from the river Taff. We had to put sacks up and planks; we were upstairs, up in the bedroom. Then you'd come down. One day I was cleaning the pantry and the rats ran over me from the river. It was terrible. The hygiene was dreadful. It was a wonder we survived. The toilet was down the bottom of the garden; no bathroom and we used to have a tub in the kitchen where we used to bath, all the children in and out. It was very primitive.

We had a cold water tap, outside. Then we had to wash with a rubbing board. I used to do the washing for all the miners. It was hard. We had a line in the back garden to dry the clothes. I don't remember what we did when it was wet: put them around the fire, probably.

I was born up the top of the valley apparently and we moved down to this house when I was nine months. It was a new house, beautiful in the front. But it was all mud, because they were still building. There was a big garden in the front, and a gate. We didn't appreciate it. We missed the pavement up the valley and the trams going up and down. Sunday morning the Salvation Army band played outside, round the corner I had an aunt and cousins, but we had to leave all of them.

ELIZABETH

It was a happy home. Mother was into the Baptist church and we were all in the Sunday School as soon as we were old enough. Four boys were born within the first ten years and a sister was born when I was twelve. My father must have been very determined that none of his sons would be going down the pit as no one did.

It must be remembered that, having a father down the station, as opposed to down the pit, made us a little different. We were expected to afford things they couldn't. It wasn't strictly true of course; we had our own economies. In this day and age I often wonder how she managed all those shirts and dresses and football kit. I still remember the bath in front of the fire, the kettle on the hob, the sheets around the fire, promptly moved when father came home. And the smell of baking bread!

In order to survive the hard times many different strategies were used to help make ends meet. When Margaret D's only brother died, her parents put the extra space to good use:

We took in lodgers, two at a time, as that was all the space we had for sleeping. It was nearly always family, because you had to share a bed in those days. It wouldn't do today, but it was family. I remember a father and son coming here from Penclawdd, and a father and son from the Rhondda, from Ferndale.

MARGARET C.

My parents had six children: three girls and three boys. She couldn't go out to work, because I mean there were six of us! And, anyway, women didn't go to work in those days. Sometimes she used to do a bit of washing, or scrub for somebody who was moving house; menial jobs for about 1/6. Before she got married, she used to scrub in a boarding house. It was a three storey house and she would scrub the bedrooms out.

35

EILEEN

My mother used to unpick coats for people, turning them and making children's coats out of them for 2/6. And very often that 2/6 came in at 6d a week.

DOROTHY

When I was twelve, I was going out picking the coal in and scrubbing the pavement, before scrubbing the house all through. When I was thirteen, I went for five weeks to look after this collier's wife who was having a baby. She had two little girls; lovely little kids they were with lovely cropped hair. But I could see them scratching a lot. I got some paper and a tooth comb and went through their hair. I never saw anything like it! They were lousy. I was only thirteen then. I got paid 15s for five weeks' work. I got food as well, but I had to do all the cooking for them, ready by the time he got home.

HAZEL

My mother had to take in washing, until she was ill, and you just lived on the goodness of your neighbours. Neighbours were fantastic in those days. We were very poor. I remember going to the soup kitchens. My sister would not go; she was disgusted. She was very proud, Muriel, a very proud young girl. They called her 'the lady'! Mother took in washing, went out cleaning and we used to go and collect the washing and take it back. I really hated it so I often got out of it. My brother today can remember that. He hated Monday, because there was always washing about the place. I did a lot of shopping. We grew up really at seven years old.

MAY

Even at that tender age we had paper rounds, I wasn't exempt any more than my brothers: it would mean an extra shilling. That shilling was mortgaged, you can say.

PHYLLIS

My mother took in a lot of washing. She did washing for a grocer and his son, which meant white coats and white aprons. She took in lodgers, and did everything you had to do for lodgers.

NANCY

My mother didn't go out to work; she worked in the garden. My father had a greenhouse, and he used to reckon that the money he earned from the sale of his chrysanthemums, which were huge big blooms, and from his tomatoes, took us on holiday every year.

ANNIE

My father kept quite a nice garden, potatoes and all the veg we wanted. He grew a lot of chrysanths, which he used to sell for 3d a bunch. He did get a job with the council, but had ill health. My mother took in my aunt's washing and ironing. She did that and she looked after her mother, occasionally.

Chapter 4

Education and Training

THIS IS NOT the place for a full scale history of education in Wales. Suffice it to say that The Fisher Education Act 1918 made secondary education compulsory up to age fourteen and gave responsibility for secondary schools to the state. However, most children attended primary (elementary) school up until age fourteen, rather than going to a separate school for secondary education. There was an opportunity for academically gifted children to win a place in a grammar school by sitting an entrance examination at the age of eleven. This test of one's abilities was traditionally known as the Scholarship and was later referred to as the Eleven Plus. Although the tuition continued to be free of charge, attending a grammar school was considered by many to be an expense beyond their reach. A grammar school education was necessary if one wanted to enter the professions and an essential move if one wanted a step up the ladder of social mobility.

When these women were in school the prevailing attitude to education was that sacrifices would be made for sons, but not for daughters. It did not matter if their daughters passed the Scholarship: it was a waste of money to send them to the grammar school as they would only end up getting married.

EILEEN

The Eleven Plus was a big thing because it meant that the boys wouldn't go down the pit because they would have a better education. My parents were very keen on this. Now, my oldest brother, he was two-and-a-half years older than me. He passed, and went to Bridgend County, as they called it. There were only seventeen months between my younger brother and me, so we both sat it the same time. I don't really know why they bothered to let me sit, because obviously they weren't going to let me go! We both passed.

Well, it was alright for the boy; they were delighted. The boys only had to have a cap and a tie and they had to have gym shorts; they liked them to have a blazer but it didn't matter if they didn't. But, you see, as a girl you had to have a gymslip, you had to have a blouse, you had to have navy blue knickers and black stockings. You had to have the hat with the badge around, with a band across and the badge. Then there was gym kit. There was a lot more uniform for girls. It was essential. I was told that girls get married and I remember crying all night, but I couldn't go.

HAZEL

I passed the exam for the grammar school, but I didn't go. It wasn't a case of not being allowed; it was a case of my mother not being able to afford to send me. You had to have school uniform in those days. You had to pay the train fare; also you had to take sandwiches to school, which wasn't on. You just accepted it.

MAY

I did go to the class where they were doing the Eleven Plus; unfortunately I wasn't able to try the exam because I had quinsy at the time. It was only once you could try, if you were in between ages and I was unfortunate to be in between. Some had a second chance, but even I didn't. But I wouldn't have been allowed to go if I had passed. There was no means for that extra, because of the uniform. My mother would be washing and getting things ready for the next day, as it was.

PHYLLIS

I came up to the school-leaving age. I was pleased that I had passed for the secondary school, but my mother said, 'Well, you won't be able to go to secondary school.'

MIRIAM

I went to Pontymaen School until I was eleven. Then we either had to try for the County School or Mill Street. Mother didn't want me to try. I ended up in Mill Street School till I was sixteen. There was nothing then for us when we left school. I left school at sixteen. I loved school. You couldn't keep me away from it. I had attendance prizes and everything. I didn't do badly in school. I think I was in the first six on the list.

ELIZABETH

I loved school and was always up with the top six. English, maths, history and music were my favourite subjects. I left my mother's English church and joined the Welsh one because they had far more singing and drama events. I won many a velvet purse, singing duets with a young lad who had a beautiful treble voice whilst I had the alto. I never missed school and hated leaving it.

I was fourteen when I left and had a year at home before being sent to London. I did not have the opportunity to sit for any further education.

MARGARET C.

I loved school. My headmistress, Miss Harris, died the other day at a hundred odd. I went to her funeral. She used to keep in touch with me because she wanted me to write. When I was in service, I always used to write to her and she would answer my letters. She was very interested in her pupils. I passed the Eleven Plus but I never even thought about going because I knew. I never reached for the stars because I knew. But I got a lot of education from being in service.

ANNIE

My father was unemployed at the time because there was a depression in the Valleys. I had to leave school at fourteen because there was no money for further education. There were nine of us in the family, four boys and five girls. I came in as the seventh child.

EUNICE

He was a very strict father and he didn't believe in education at all for girls, not for boys even. I did pass the Eleven Plus, as it was in those days, but he wouldn't let me go to grammar school. He said that he couldn't afford it – but I was the last and the others were working. He could have really if he had wanted to. I went back to the ordinary school until I was fourteen. I would have liked to have gone on and been a domestic science teacher, but it wasn't to be and it's no good being bitter about it, is it?

There were sometimes more pressing reasons for leaving school and although there were attendance officers employed to check that children went to school regularly, it appears that sometimes they turned a blind eye.

MARY K.

I loved school. Even when the snow was deep, deep, I went. But there were days when I had to stay home. My mother said, 'You've got to stop home today to look after Vi.' I'd miss history and it was dreadful. I went back to school and I didn't know the answers. I loved school. I left at eleven because I had a sister with meningitis and she was dying, and there were no hospitals to take her. There was one younger, so I had to stay and look after the baby, I didn't get any more schooling.

Morddfa passed the Eleven Plus and went to secondary school in Ogmore Vale, but left at fourteen because she had chest trouble. When her mother died, she had to stay home to care for the family.

Dorothy had her own very personal reasons for wanting to leave school:

> There used to be a pebble yard, a concrete yard at school. My mother had very little money coming in and the other girls used to wear little shoes, but I wore boots with steel caps. I used to feel rather embarrassed when I walked round the yard; I was making more noise than other people. They used to wear little white blouses and mother had made us blouses, butcher's blue, with white stripes. I used to want to wear white blouses like the others. Mother couldn't afford it. The headmaster sent for my father and said that he thought that I should stay on at school, because I would get on well with my exams. I was adamant! No! I was going to leave and I was going to be a cook. I looked at Mrs Beeton's cookery book that my mother had. I used to sit and look at the plates, the coloured pictures, and I decided that I wanted to be a cook.

Some of them realised their limitations and were happy to leave school when the time came. Doris was quite phlegmatic in her reasons for not furthering her education:

> I didn't take the Eleven Plus. My sister, who was two years older than me, they put her up for this special test and she used to come home and she used to cry her eyes out, so they wouldn't let me do it. They'd had enough with her! She didn't pass and I think she was a little brighter than me.

HILDA

I went to the local school, Dyffryn in Ferndale, for about ten years, leaving at the age of fourteen. You went through school and then you sat for secondary school. I didn't seem to be that way inclined, so I left school at fourteen, like most of us did.

MARGARET D.

I went to the elementary school in Cwmcrach, after I left school then, no work of course. I didn't have a lot upstairs. I hated school. I was fourteen when I left school.

In order to prepare these young girls for life outside school, in some cases attempts were made to help them with their future employment.

MARGARET C.
Before I left school at fourteen, we used to have lessons in domestic science. We used to go to cookery class and we went to laundry.

EUNICE
We had cookery lessons and also one teacher who was a great one for teaching you how to sew, which came in handy because I made all my own clothes. When my daughters were born, I was able to make their clothes. She was very good really, she was an excellent teacher. I enjoyed school, I must say.

HAZEL
I stayed in Blaenllynfi School. They built a special bungalow in the school grounds, where they taught us basic housework and cooking. Once the girls from the other two local schools turned eleven, they came down to our school to learn domestic service, as well as learning the basic things.

However my mother couldn't afford to give me the ingredients. We didn't know what a fresh egg was. Milk? We never had fresh milk until they had it in the school. They started to bring a third of a pint of milk in. That was a penny a week or two pence a week and I helped to pay for that with the pocket money I earned. Otherwise it was condensed milk and that's why I don't take sugar today, because I hated it.

Other girls did not get any training at school but felt confident that their mothers had prepared them for domestic work outside the home.

EUNICE
I didn't learn that type of cooking at school. My mother had taught the four of us, my two brothers as well. She'd even taught them to patch and sew buttons on! It was the done

43

A perfect mix: learning to cook at Lapswood.
(Getty Images)

thing in those days, you see. You learnt all this before you left school.

The Government sponsored training schemes for girls in unemployment black spots and three of the women had attended them. Margaret D. gave me a vivid account of her time spent in Lapswood, Sydenham Hill, London.

MARGARET D.

I went to London then, sixteen I was, into service. It was to Lapswood, this training place in Sydenham Hill, SE26.

We went to London because all the girls were going there, so you had to follow suit, see. 'So and so's going to London, to that Lapswood place.' It was all we knew.

My parents didn't have to pay for us to go. It was part of a Labour Exchange scheme, and started with a stiff medical in Neath. You didn't know if you had TB back then, after all. Then you got a letter informing you whether you'd been accepted or not. It was off to this big house, then. Three months training it was. Oooh, it was training too mind. There were no carpets or anything; we had to go on our knees to scrub these boards white. It was training you see, for domestic work and we all knew what was domestic work was, because we were nearly all domestics! I think there were one or two from Gloucester there and the others were all Welsh girls. From down the west, from Brynaman and Garnant and the like, mostly they were. Others followed from the village then, after us. Crowds went, about fifteen altogether. Eventually we were all scattered around London. I went to Chiswick when I finished.

I learnt to cook there as well. You had a week in the laundry, a week in cooking, a week in the sewing room. (I don't know why we wanted that for, because I didn't know how to hold a needle tidy, to sew!) Then a week as acting parlour maid, for the staff. It was promotion for you, all clean work. You had to change to black and white in the afternoon, and answer bells. I learnt to answer the telephone and the door properly, in readiness to go out to service, to go out to gentry.

In the evening you were free, at least you were after the laundry and cooking lectures that took place after supper. Of course it was lights out at eleven o'clock, but you would be laughing and joking until the maid came and knocked the door. There were lots of us there, you see; thirty or forty girls. It was a big house.

I wrote to my mother once a week, sometimes twice. She always knew when I had the old Welsh 'hiraeth', because she would receive more than one letter. You wouldn't show that you had this 'hiraeth' of course. You just wrote to every Tom, Dick and Harry, just to have letters back, d'you see? I remember having one letter back from a friend who said, 'It's dead here. They call it the bachelor village now. All the girls have gone to Lapswood.'

When any new girls arrived at Lapswood they were not shown any sympathy by the earlier recruits:

MARGARET D.
I was very homesick when we went. Everybody was, you know. When the new girls would come in, we'd be laughing at them saying, 'You'll get over that. We were all like that.' We were terribly homesick but we wouldn't show see because they would say, 'Serve you right for going. You didn't have to go.' But it was training, good training, hard training. You knew what you had to do and the staff had everything to perfection, as though you were in service. You had to wait on them. 'To take away with the left and serve with the right' – I'll always remember that.

Two more of the interviewees went to the local training establishment in Pontypridd. It was held in a large house called Jacobsdale which has since been demolished.

ANNIE
I couldn't have further education for financial reasons, so I went to a training centre, linked to a school for those with unemployed fathers, to do seventeen weeks' training. This

Domestic Godesses: learning to scrub at Lapswood.
(Getty Images)

covered laundry, cookery, chambermaid, parlour maid and answering the door and the telephone in the proper manner. They guaranteed you a job at the end of seventeen weeks of training.

It really was like *Upstairs, Downstairs*. We absolutely lived like ladies because the cooks did their job and the parlour maids did their job. If we were training in housewifery or laundry, when the dinner bell went, we sat down to our food as if we were real ladies. The parlour maids had to lay the tables in the proper manner, which was an experience for them; they had to learn to serve properly. The only thing I didn't like was the one meal on Friday. It was steamed cod and parsley sauce, but it was prunes and junket afterwards; that was just milk and essence of rennet. Very good for you!

We had to sleep in whilst I was training, for one week, to get used to being away from home. That was a rather good idea. It was in a big house, which I think was called Jacobsdale. We took it in turns to do all the different things. A week on the laundry; a week on housewifery; a week on sewing; a week on cooking; a week on staff cooking; a week on chambermaids.

MIRIAM

There was this house Jacobsdale up at Lanwood which they turned into a domestic place where they taught you how to be a domestic servant, and then they found you a job. That's how I ended up in service. We didn't have to pay to go, that was an offer they gave us. We did six months there and they'd find us a job. They gave you the basics. I went as a chambermaid when I went out to service. People used to write there for domestics. They used to pay the train fare, up to Ascot in my case. They had given us our uniforms at Jacobsdale. They gave us the blue frock, white apron, that's all and a mob cap.

I also met another lady in Cardiff called Amy who at aged ninety, in 2006, was able to remember her time in Jacobsdale. She lived in a village some eight miles from Pontypridd and remembered being given the train fare and some pocket money to attend. She told me that thirty girls attended at any one time and there were ten in a class. They were taught housework, laundry and cooking and she also remembered the last week being residential. She was found a job with a stockbroker in Bromley, Kent. Their chauffeur met her at Paddington and kindly gave her a little tour of London before taking her to her destination. Amy was reluctant to leave home and wanted to get off the train at Newport, the station after Cardiff where she had boarded the train, as she was so unhappy. Times were hard for her family in the General Strike and to prevent their shoes from leaking in the winter, her mother would put cardboard in them. Later, the schoolmaster organised a delivery of boots for the whole school.

Although some of the girls were prepared for their future life, many were still very young and totally inexperienced.

MAY

I wasn't trained in anything in school. I was doing arithmetic on the Friday afternoon and I was away on the Saturday. It was cruel. There was no advance warning; all that we knew was once we came to fourteen, we had to go away from home, because there was not a penny coming in to keep us.

Chapter 5

Finding Work and Leaving Home

LOCAL NEWSPAPERS carried hundreds of advertisements for domestic servants, but only a couple of those interviewed got work this way. It was considered better, safer, to use family connections – recommendations by friends and relatives already away. The employer would ask for references and the head teacher, or better still, the local minister would supply them. But there was no way for the girl to know what her employers would be like, unless she knew someone already working there. It was a total leap into the dark.

EILEEN

My mother knew that I was leaving school in the December and she had written to one of the ladies, a Miss Greener, where she used to work. (She always sent us a Christmas card.) She wrote asking if she knew of a place for me to go to. Miss Greener was in her opinion a wonderful person, and she wrote back. She had spent time out in South Africa, and had got to know a Captain Cornwall and his wife and the family. He was a retired captain of police in South Africa. She told my mother in the letter she had only met them once, but she knew they were looking for a girl. She gave my mother this address, which was in a place called Brympton, near Reading. My mother wrote there and this was before I had actually left school. This lady had written back and told my mother everything she wanted, what uniform I had to have, and that it would be 10s a week.

DOMESTIC SERVANTS WANTED.

KITCHENMAID, single hand, wanted at once; aged 17 to 19 years; country. Apply Box 15, "Free Press," Pontypridd.

GENERAL, about 30, good plain cooking; housework; no stairs or steps; family two. —Mrs. Edkins, Flat A 30, Greencroft-gardens, Finchley-road, London.

GENERAL, for Cardiff; experienced; good refernces; aged 25-30.—Apply, Box 11, "Free Press," Pontypridd.

GENERAL MAID for small, easy, modern house; good plain cooking required; man for boots and coal; good references essential, £50. Apply, "W," Burrswood, Upland-road, Sutton, Surrey.

WILLING maid for Pontypridd; good home and training. Apply, B.A., "Free Press," Pontypridd.

SUPERIOR Girl, beginner, for good domestic service; no kitchen work. Address, Mrs. W., care of newsagents, 198, Ebury-street, London, S.W.1.

CAPABLE General maid; family four; good wages; references. Apply, 40, Richmond-road, Cardiff.

Reading between the lines: situations vacant for girls.

DOROTHY

I had an aunt in London, working with some Maltese people, in a big three-storey house. She wrote to Mamma. I had to get work. My mother couldn't afford to keep me. She said that they wanted a kitchen maid. 'Could Dorothy come up as a kitchen maid?' Going to London, going to my aunt, I was quite excited about it. I thought it would be nice. My mother got my clothes ready. Dad took me to Cardiff and put me on the train, and my aunt met me the other end and took me down to the job. There was a cook there. My aunt was parlour maid and they had a man there, a butler, and myself, the kitchen maid.

HAZEL

My godmother, Aunty Frances, had a step-daughter who worked for the Rothschilds in Rickmansworth. Their cousin in London wanted a kitchen maid. I had the job automatically, so we had to get my uniform. There was a shop in Maesteg. Mother and I walked the two-and-a-half miles to Maesteg, bought a suitcase; bought the uniform; called in on a friend's mother on the way back to have a drink, and then walked the rest of the way home.

I was bitterly disappointed that I didn't have a new coat or a new dress. We had a second-hand one from Mrs Jones at no. 14's daughter, who was a house maid to Lord and Lady Nuffield. She was marrying one of the men who worked in the factory and theirs was the first car we ever saw in Caerau. Annie got married and it was Annie's clothes I had to go to London.

PHYLLIS

I hadn't been home long when I went back up to London. I got a job in a club because a friend of mine from Newport had recommended this place, where she was working. It was a very big club in Charing Cross called St James's Constitutional; a businessmen's club, a very big place. It was residential for men. Our quarters were on the opposite side of the road. I was taken on.

MARY K.

When I was looking after my sister, she knew I was looking for a job, and reminded me that I had a cousin in Basingstoke. He was a warden in a mental hospital. My sister said, 'There's a job going for you.'

EILEEN

My granny took me back to the Isle of Wight with her. The daughter of a friend of hers was working for a doctor in Cowes and knew that the other doctor was looking for a girl. I went down to see this doctor Balfour and his wife and little baby. He was Scottish, she was an American and and they were only in their thirties, much younger than the other people that I'd worked for.

HILDA

When I was seventeen, things became very bad underground. It would have been about 1930, I suppose. Some days they worked and some days they were not able to work. I wanted to help and, like most girls in the same situation, we had no alternative but to go to seek work elsewhere. We weren't trained for anything really, having left school at fourteen, but we knew how to work domestically, so we found work away from the Valleys. That's all we could do really. We didn't know anything else.

My cousin from Maerdy was a little older and she was already away. She said that there was a place for me, at the Red House in Surrey, if I would like to come. So I went to Surrey as an under housemaid.

Her second job was also secured through a friend, this time on the spot!

Then the village postman, from Surrey, wrote to me and said there was a vacancy at the big manor house, if I would like to apply. I had kept in touch with him, made friends. The postman was your best friend when you're away from home because you look forward to a letter, don't you? I welcomed a letter. It was great. Sometimes my mother would send me Welsh cakes! They were still in one piece; they knew how to pack in those days. The postman was more careful and would come around on a bicycle.

He wrote to me. I applied for this other job. That was under parlour maid; another trip to London. I was met at Dorking Station. They had a car and they met me and took me home.

PHYLLIS

When I went home I found that two of my sisters were working in Newport, in different places. My sister phoned up then to say I could have a job in the same street as her. This is my oldest sister now; she'd gone back to service. She said, 'You can have a job with an old lady living down the street. I'll be able to see you everyday. You'll be able to come up to my place.' Her people ran a little grocery business and they were very nice to her. They had a little girl and boy.

My next move from there was through my other sister. She said that a friend of her Mrs was the landlady of the big Ship Hotel in Newport. I went for a job there, and I got it. You could easily get jobs because they were always looking out for maids.

In some villages there was a local agent who fixed them up, for a fee, and a lady from Merthyr told me that she remembered a Jewish lady finding jobs for local girls with Jewish families in London.

CEINWEN

Mrs Knight of Tydixton Court, on the way to Porthcawl, used to find jobs for people so I went up there with my half sister, who was always with me, and we went to see her and she got me the job. I was about fourteen when I went to London. My mother didn't want me to go, but we just had to go. We weren't allowed to stay at home. Mrs Knight kitted you out in the uniform. And I went to work for the Duchess of Grafton. I was a kitchen maid.

MAY

There was a lady in Treorchy who found the job; she was an agent. She always managed to get work for girls away from home, whether it was a club or anything else. My mother must have approached her; it wouldn't have been my father, because he wouldn't have parted with us. My mother found it difficult enough, mind you.

Another lady came around and she used to spend a day sewing. She was paid by the day, not much, and was given food. That was when the front room was used and we had to have three dresses. I can see it now: pinstriped pink and white, little Peter Pan collars and white aprons, with caps. I thought I was going to be very posh in this outfit. I had to have a suitcase, but I can't remember whether the case was new or not. I doubt it. It must have been second-hand or handed down.

MARY W.

I went to Pontypridd, to this agency, and they got me this job as a scullery maid in a house between Shaftesbury and Blandford. There were ten servants, three house maids, a housekeeper, a kitchen maid, a scullery maid a French governess for the one daughter, a footman and a butler.

DORIS

I stayed in school until I was nearly fifteen. Then I decided that I wanted to go away so I wrote to an agency. I think it was in the Somerset area, and they sent me a few lists of jobs. I wrote to this one in Malvern, West Malvern, which was a girls' college. I had to have three references. I got one from the chapel, one from this Aunty Price, who I had done shopping for, and the music teacher, who we knew very well. I had to go for an interview, up to West Malvern. I think my mother went with me. Anyway I got the job, so I started there, leaving home for the first time.

Copy Reference for
Blaengwrach School

was a pupil at the above School throughout her school life. We found her honest, straightforward, neat & tidy in appearance and she always gave of her best. It gives me pleasure to give her this testimonial as I am sure she will give every satisfaction

(Teacher)

Blaengwrach school gives its seal of approval to a former pupil.

(Glamorgan Archives)

At nineteen Morddfa fell out with her father and went to London into service. When her mother died, she had to stay home to care for the family. Her older brothers were already working in the colliery. She had to get up early to cut their snap boxes and fill their jacks with homemade barley water. Often her brothers' clothes would be damp so these had to be aired, and their breakfast made before they left for work. They worked shifts so her work was non-stop. Her father gave her one shilling a week pay. She went away because she wanted some independence and an existence of her own. She had heard that her cousins from the Rhondda had gone into service to London and had done well there. She wanted to go to London to see some life outside the village. Although she belonged to local choirs and went to concerts in the village, she yearned for more. She had found the job through a woman in the village. The agent was paid 2/6 and then she found positions for the local girls.

Newspapers and magazines did play a role and several of the women applied for posts through this traditional route.

NELLIE

The job was advertised in the *Argus*, when I went to the Herbert Street Nursing home. I was there quite a while.

MARGARET C.

One day there was this article written, in the *Daily Express*, round about 1927–1928, about the hardships of the coloured girls in Bute Town. It was hard for them to get jobs. But it wasn't only the coloured girls, it was the white as well. This lady in Penally, saw it in the paper and she wrote to the *Daily Express*. Mrs Ellwood was her name. They sent her a few names and addresses. We all had to write and she picked me out to try. She chose me. I went with her. She offered me wages of 4s a week.

NANCY

My mother took the *Nursing Mirror and Midwives Journal* for several weeks. She looked through the adverts until she found a situation for a house maid, in a nursing home.

June 7th 1940

Madam.

In reply to your advertisement for a House Maid in the Western Mail on the 6th I wish to apply for the Post I am 17 years old and I have had no previous experience.

Should you wish an interview I shall be pleased to oblige at your convenience when the matter of wages could be discussed.

Reference will follow later

Your obedient

Seventeen years old, and ready for work: a reply to a newspaper advertisement.

(Glamorgan Archives)

EUNICE

My mother found the post for me in Wiltshire. I don't know how. I was suddenly told I had to go. We went off and bought a little cardboard case and uniform and that was it. Off I had to go. You obeyed your parents in those days. You just didn't say, 'Oh, I don't want to do that!' That would have been the end. You were put on the train and off you went. You didn't know where you were going or who was going to meet you. It was terrible. My sister was the same, going up to London.

MEGAN

When I became fourteen in March, there was nothing left, only to go to service. Some of my friends were lucky enough to get odd jobs in the village.

DORIS

When I came home I looked for another job. I wrote to this house in Chepstow. It must have been advertised; I'm not sure where I got the information from. I wrote to this person in Chepstow and she wanted me to meet her in Newport. My sister and myself went to Newport somewhere to have this interview. I don't remember where I went. Anyway I got the job. It was in a gentleman's house.

Megan had no choice when she came home after her stint of holiday cleaning in the boys' school in Malvern. She was packed off to London with her aunty:

I had this month's money when I come home and my mother got me a job with my aunty. When I came from Malvern, then we went to London. I shall always remember thinking, 'Oooh I shall see the Queen!' I thought the Queen was a wonderful thing. Well, we went to Putney Hill and their name was Sparkes and they had ten daughters, but there was only four of them left. They were that old-fashioned; well it was not like Victorian times, it was worse than that.

Phyllis did an exchange with her sister, who was needed at home by her mother who unbeknown to Phyllis was about to have a baby:

I saw the tin trunk and the bed being brought down to the front room. I was at a curious age and had an idea that my mother was having a baby. I was too young to know. She made all the napkins, out of Turkish towel. She stitched them all on the old machine. As soon as somebody come in, she'd stick them under the machine, put the lid on so nobody would know, right up until the time I went away. She said to me, 'You can't go to secondary school, because Lizzie …' (that was

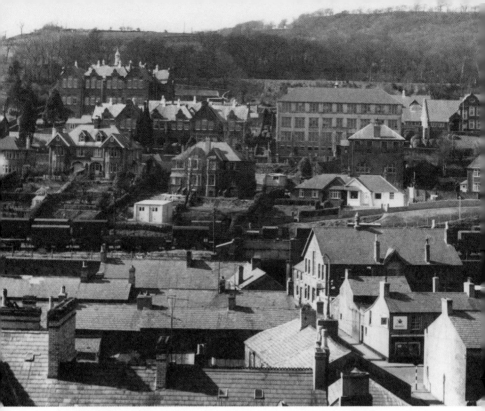

Jacobsdale in Pontypridd, a government training establishment where would-be servants were trained. (Rhondda Cynon Taf Library Services)

my older sister who had got a job in London and was working for Jewish people there.) '… Lizzie has got to come home for a rest', she said, 'Because she's not well. I want you to go up and take her place until she's better.' That was supposed to be the understanding.

After Annie finished her training at Jacobsdale she had to take the job that she was offered as that was part of the deal:

My first job after my training was with Dr Gray in Grangetown, Cardiff. Dad took me down for the interview. The cook accepted me and was very pleased. I went as a cook assistant because I was really interested in cooking.

For the more adventurous girl there were opportunities further afield than London. An advertisement in *The Free Press of*

Monmouthshire dated 29 July 1927 asked for girls to go out to Australia under the auspices of the Salvation Army.

> The Salvation Army has chartered the White Star line *Vedic* to sail to Australia with a company of prospective settlers on Saturday, October 15th . . . Young women, experienced and inexperienced, willing to undertake household duties, are in much demand in Australia, and for those who place themselves under their care the Army guarantees situations at good wages. The living conditions in Australia are stated to be extremely comfortable. Free passages will be given to approved experienced domestics, while suitable domesticated women, inexperienced, but willing to do housework, will be granted nominated passages for which the rate is £16. 10s, which will be repayable by monthly instalments out of wages. This money, however, will be returned to the young women at the end of twelve months provided they have completed a year's domestic service satisfactorily.
>
> The *Vedic*, which is a well-appointed ship, will be specially equipped for the Salvation Army Company. The social side will be under the direction of men and women officers experienced in migration work, and under the Army protection any young woman who makes the adventure should have a great sense of security as while travelling anywhere at home. She will be well looked after.
>
> The fare on board will be plentiful and wholesome. There will be a dry canteen, but no intoxicating liquor will be sold on board. An orchestra will be in the ship to provide music for the company, while organised community singing and other forms of amusements have been promised.
>
> The *Vedic*, besides the company of domestics, will take a number of boys, single young men and families to Australia.

Once the job was determined, then the necessary preparations were made for departure, the most important aspect being to acquire the uniform. In some instances the employer would advance the cost of the uniform and the rail fare to the parents, to be deducted from the wages later. Some mothers made the uniform themselves or the local sewing woman came in and made it. Viscount Tonypandy and former Speaker of the House of Commons the late George Thomas's mother was such a sewing woman when they were on hard times. There were shops too that specialised in maids' outfits, like the one Hazel remembered in Maesteg. The uniform consisted of a cotton dress – pink or blue, with a white apron and cap. Those who became parlour maids, or who worked all through the house, and not just in the kitchen, had to have a black afternoon dress and a small lace cap too. Dorothy told me:

> When I first left home my mother got me the pink dress and white aprons, and a canvas one for all my scrubbing. They weren't supplied. My mother's sister was staying with us and she was a dressmaker. I think she made them for me.

> MEGAN
> I always remember my mother having a beautiful pair of linen sheets. She cut them up to make some aprons for the morning, and she made some little ones for the afternoon and put some laces around them. I had to have one cap for the morning and a fancy cap for the afternoon. My mother cut a handkerchief in two and bound it around and she put a bit of black ribbon through it, then she embroidered around it with a bit of lace.

> HILDA
> I remember the day I left, although nothing much was done in the way of preparation. You had to have a blue dress and a couple of aprons and that, and plenty of underwear. My parents came with me to Cardiff Station. I went from there then to Paddington, where I was met, which made it easier, didn't it? The second time I wasn't. Then we drove right out into the country.

> ELIZABETH
> Without much preamble, I was suddenly buying new clothes with my mother, not really understanding the need, but loving my father and somehow trusting him to do what he

considered the best thing for me. My journey was planned and off I went to Kensington Gore, London, to the home of Mr John Tilling. I was not asked if I wanted to go away, but accepted it quite happily, perhaps without being conscious of it. I too wanted to get away from the enclosing mountains, where there were no other prospects.

I was put in the care of one guard from Maerdy to Cardiff, and passed on to the guard on the London Train, each one knowing my father of course. I was eventually handed over to the housekeeper of Mr Tilling's household. She was very kind and took great care of me.

EILEEN

I left school at the Christmas and in the January it was arranged for me to go to this place in Reading. My mother took me to Cardiff and put me on the train, which stopped at Reading. I had my case. My mother had made two blue overalls, a big white overall, to go over it and a white mop cap that covered my head. Then for the afternoon I had to have a black dress and a little white pinny and a different headdress. So I had 2/6 in my pocket and my ticket.

The great adventure started with the train journey to the new place of work, usually London. For young girls who had never been far from home, perhaps just to the seaside for the day with the Sunday school, the journey itself was traumatic and was only the prelude to what lay ahead. In all cases arrangements were made to meet the girls at the railway station.

MIRIAM

I never take anybody to the station when I go anywhere. 'You leave me. You stop here and I'll go.' I can remember leaving Pontypridd then we had to change at Reading then, over to the other line, to go to Ascot, all on the GWR. They picked me up at Ascot, took me there. For the first fortnight I was terribly homesick. Ooh! I was terribly homesick. I hadn't left home before. Once I got over that fortnight I was alright.

CEINWEN

My father saw me off at the station. I was sobbing my heart out as soon as the train left the station. One woman wanted to call him, to fetch me home. I nearly broke my heart, I did. I'd never been to London. I didn't know what to expect, did I? And I swore that if ever I got married, my children would never do it. Never! They would never skivvy for anybody else, and thank God they didn't have to.

I can't remember anyone meeting me at Paddington, but there must have been someone there. I was the only Welsh girl in the house and they couldn't pronounce my name, so I went as 'Jane'. Every letter I'd have from home I used to take to the toilet where I'd be sobbing my heart out. My mother used to say, 'Be a brave girl.' But I broke my heart, I did. I'd never wish it on anybody.

Ceinwen was fourteen years old when she left home. So was May and it appears that neither she nor her sister ever fully recovered from the trauma.

MAY

I remember the day I left. Oh dear! I went down to Cardiff with my brother and then from there up to London. I said 'Good-bye' to my mother here in the house. It wasn't until years afterwards my brother told me: 'Do you know that Mam collapsed before you had reached the corner. She had kept being brave, showing you that it was something that everybody else was doing, but she collapsed.' I asked my sister, 'What did you feel, Nance, when you left home? What was the homesickness like?' She said, 'I remember it now. I was so scarred that no doctor could have made such a deep scar.' Nance was ninety-five when she said this; she had never forgotten. She'd been dreadful, worse for her because she was leaving us all. She was our second mother. What Nance said, went.

HAZEL

Mother took me to Cardiff. I had put a little white flower in the lapel of my coat. I can see it now, a sort of a bluey-grey coat, and I had a 1920s hat and flat shoes. Horrid. I was met in London by Aunty Lillian, as I called her. She was housekeeper to the Rothschilds. She took me over to Ormes Square in Bayswater.

I didn't cry on the train like some of the girls. No, I thought I was never ever homesick, until when I think back. I was never so homesick as to cry, because they all remarked on it: 'You didn't cry!' No, to me I was now being fed. I had good meals.

MARGARET C.

I was upset at leaving home. The morning I left home, I didn't have any money. I got on the train and it was a long journey, because I didn't know where I was going. Penally. Nobody seemed to know where it was. She said, 'When you come to Penally, wear a flower in your coat, so I will know you. I got off the train. Miss Whitely and Mrs Ellwood were meeting me. They said, 'You're Margaret?' I said. 'Yes'. And Mrs Ellwood said, 'Come along and we'll have a cup of tea.' It was a great big place. 'Fern House' it was called. It was a lovely house. We went and had tea. Well, I got there about three o'clock I think. I must have left home about eleven. They only lived right by the station.

PHYLLIS

I went to London at fourteen-and-a-half. My mother took me down to Cardiff in the train. I got off at Paddington where my sister was going to meet me. I saw the passengers getting off – but no sister! So I found my own way, by asking; asking drivers and different people, how to get to Aldgate and finally I got there and found the address. My sister was working for milliners, she had come up to meet me, but we had missed each other, so she was left crying on Paddington Station!

As soon as I went in the new house, the first thing the girls in the work shop asked was, 'Has your mother had the baby yet? I said, 'I don't know.' Eventually they made a fuss of me and my sister found her way back in tears. Almost the first thing she did was shorten my clothes. She said, 'They'll have to come up.' She stayed with me for a few days, to give me the run of the place.

Mary W. chose to identify herself at Paddington by wearing a cap of many colours. As a result, the Jewish family for whom she subsequently worked always called her 'Jo'. She had been so brainwashed by the stories at home of the white slave trade that she was too afraid to speak to the man who approached her on the platform, who unbeknown to her at this point, was her prospective employer.

MARY W.

I don't know how they got this job in London for me, but it was the most awful experience. I didn't know where I was going. They sent me an 8/- day return ticket. They were Jews and they sent a letter telling me to write to say what I was dressed in and they'd meet me at the station.

Nobody came with me to the bus. I got lost. I got off at Queen Street station instead of the General Station in Cardiff. When I got to the right station, the excursion train was going. I was running after it. A shilling I had, no food, nothing. I had my period at the time: I felt terrible.

I said to the porter. 'I'm supposed to be on that train. I've got my ticket.' He said, 'Go into the office.' I was in tears. 'Where are you supposed to go?' I said, 'Here's the address. I don't know where it is.' He said, 'I'll tell you what. You sit here.' They must have phoned through for me. They said, 'Wait now until the ordinary train comes.' I could go on that with my ticket. It was getting dark by now and I didn't have anything to eat, nothing to drink. I felt sick.

I got into the compartment and there was a lady in the corner. I can see her now: she had a serviette with finger sandwiches.

I was just sitting there and she was looking at me and she said, 'Would you like a sandwich, my dear?' 'Yes please', I said. She gave me a few little sandwiches, so that lasted me.

The thing was now that I was supposed to be met on Paddington Station. I wasn't to speak to any men. It was pitch dark. I got the fright of my life. I wrote on the letter – I shall be on Paddington Station and I'll have on a cap of many colours and a navy coat.' Right. Up comes a man, big, stout. 'Excuse me', he said, 'are you Mary?' 'I'm not speaking to you,' I thought. White slaves were about in those days. I looked at him again and thought, 'I don't like the look of him. I've got my return ticket.' I was safe. I thought I could go back on the midnight train, all the way to Beddau. He said, 'I've come to meet you.' I thought, 'Well, I don't know. I'm not going to answer.' I was getting more nervous by the minute, but there were lots of people about. He can't do anything at all. All of a sudden, up comes a lady, running. It was his sister. He said, 'I've found her, but she's deaf and dumb!'

She was lovely. She said, 'Hello'. 'Hello' I said. 'He's quite harmless, my dear. He's my brother.' They were poor, honestly 7/6 a week! She said, 'I've got to go back to the office.' 'Oh, have you?' I got frightened again now. I thought there might be some twist. 'Master Jack will take you.' I said, 'Really?' 'Yes, he's quite harmless, really.' I still had my eye on him.

Mary W. was then escorted to their home in the Shadwell Dock, in the East End, which would have appeared to her as exotic as the Far East, full of immigrants – not known to her in her native Rhondda:

Here he goes now into a train, from Paddington, right down to Liverpool Street and, off there. Then he went down a side street. He wanted to go to the loo. I thought, 'Now is my chance to run away.' It was a dark, horrible street, near Whitechapel it was. I was on the pavement with my little case and I thought, 'I don't like this place, I think I'll go to the police.' I was that desperate, but I didn't get a chance, he caught me by the

arm. I said, 'Where are we going now?' He said, 'The tram.'
Trains, tram, a bus, I don't know. We came right into Stepney,
Commercial Road it was. We got off there now and there was
this alley way, right down to Shadwell Dock.

Down we went to a terrace there, in we go now and there's
a dad there with a black hat on. There was a married daughter
and her husband; he was a lorry driver. There was a little girl
about three, sweet little thing, she was. And there was the
other sister, the one who met me. She was working up in the
West End, in an office. That was the family all together, five
of them.

In addition to the young girls being very distressed at leaving
home, their parents too found the whole experience heart rending.
In three cases the women said that it was their fathers that did not
want them to go away. Margaret C.'s father sat in his chair and cried
when he got back from the station, whilst Nancy's father seemed
more concerned that her moral welfare was at risk whilst working
in a nursing home. Her mother had bought her a party frock for her
birthday and then she wrote and said:

> 'Will you give it away please. I have never known your father
> to be so upset about anything I have bought, in the whole of
> my married life.' He thought I would be in my party frock
> and dashing off to wherever there was to go! The fact was that
> I only got a half-day once a week and that didn't start until
> two o'clock and then I had to be in at half-past nine. I got a
> weekend once a month and then I went home. There wasn't
> much time for partying!

Although he was not able to save his family of nine children from
the ravages of poverty, Miriam's father, a stone cutter in Pontypridd,
was reluctant to part with any of his children:

> I remember the day I left Pontypridd, I broke my heart! I can
> remember sitting up in bed. My mother used to have cats and
> I was sitting with one cat in one arm and one cat in the other

and my father came up to kiss me goodbye. He didn't want me to go. He didn't want any of his children to leave home, but there was nothing for us. I mean the government didn't give you money to look after you then. I was sitting up in bed and I was breaking my heart.

Of all the feelings that the women expressed, it was those concerning homesickness that were the most poignant. Twelve of the twenty described to me their feelings of depression.

MARGARET C.
So I laid the table. She told me how many to lay for. Then it smelt lovely and it was all ready and she got me to carry all the dishes in. She said grace and I couldn't stop crying. She got up and said, 'We'll take you back in the kitchen.' She said, 'Now sit in here until you stop crying.' I think I cried all night and I couldn't eat anything.

ANNIE
I was very homesick when I first left home. I wanted to run back home because I missed the good breakfast in the morning. Because money was tight Mother used to go down to the Co-op. You know when they slice bacon on the machine, there was a lot of bits spare, so my mum would buy quite a lot of those bits. Sometimes you'd get big pieces in there. We used to have porridge first, that was a must and then we had either bacon and fried bread and fried apple, which was beautiful, absolutely lovely. It was like gammon and pineapple, but far nicer.

Ceinwen was permanently homesick the whole two years she spent in London. May told me that although she was a regular chapel goer at home, she couldn't bear to go in London as hearing them all speak Welsh made her long for home too much. As the sole servant in a house in Melksham, Eunice at fourteen was particularly lonely:

I was terribly homesick. I used to sit on the stairs and cry with the dog. It was awful. I think my sister was the same. On your half day off and your day off on a Sunday, it was absolute agony. I did eventually get friendly with a farmer and his wife. They had a smallholding and I was able to go there which was rather nice. But I was terribly homesick. Melksham was a very tiny place.

Not all the contributors suffered in this way. Hilda cried for the first month, Miriam only cried for a fortnight. Once Elizabeth understood what was required of her, she began to enjoy herself. At first, Hazel denied that she had been at all homesick:

I was never homesick as to cry, because they all remarked on it. But to me, I was now being fed. I had good meals.

Later , however, she was to admit that she must have been a little homesick:

In a way I suppose I was, because I often walked to Paddington Station and watched the trains come in, just to hear the Welsh accents.

There were definite advantages in having other members of the family nearby.

MARY K.
My sister came up too. She was crying all the time. I had to look after her. I'd be on duty at the hotel, and I'd have a phone call. She was crying. It kept on and on. I said, 'I'm going to put you on the train and send you back home.' She said. 'I don't want to go home, because there's nothing at home, nothing, really.'

Then I went up to where she was working, in a house on her own. She was lonely. So the lady said to me, 'I wonder if you would work for me?' 'No.' I said, 'I work in a hotel. My sister is homesick. I think I'll send her home.' But she wouldn't go. My other sister came up and they got to be scullery maids in big houses. Lord and Lady Astor I think it was, that's where they went.

CEINWEN

On my half day off I used to go to Kilburn to see my mother's sister. I stayed in London for two years and my aunt wrote to my mother and said, 'If you don't want that girl to have a breakdown, then you have to have her home.'

I nearly broke my heart. I was awfully homesick for two years.

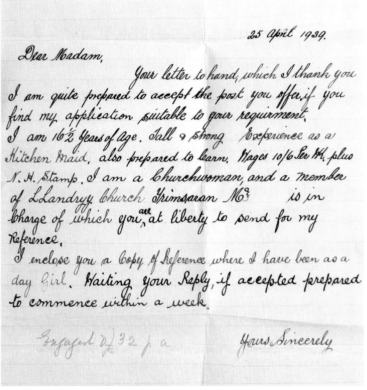

25 April 1939.

Dear Madam,

Your letter to hand, which I thank you I am quite prepared to accept the post you offer if you find my application suitable to your requirment. I am 16½ Years of Age. Tall & Strong Experience as a Kitchen maid, also prepared to learn. Wages 10/6 Per Wk, plus N.H. Stamp. I am a Churchwoman, and a member of LLandryy Church Trimsaran No? is in Charge of which you are at liberty to send for my Reference. I enclose you a Copy of Reference where I have been as a day Girl. Waiting your Reply, if accepted prepared to commence within a week.

Engaged D/ 32 p a

Yours Sincerely

'I am quite prepared to accept the post'. No turning back now!

(Glamorgan Archives)

Chapter 6

What the Job Entailed

THERE WAS A distinct hierarchy in the field of domestic service and by the very nature of their age and inexperience, my contributors started at the very bottom of the ladder. In a large household there would be six or seven servants. 'Large' does not relate to the number of people living in the house, only to the wealth and status of its occupants. Ceinwen was completely overawed working for the Duchess of Grafton, in Princess Gate.

CEINWEN

The house was in Princes Gate in Kensington and there was a butler, chauffeur, parlour maid, house maid, cook and me. We all lived in, down in the basement. The housekeeper was in charge of running the house. There was no Duke living in Princes Gate. He was the nephew and he never lived there. But the Duchess lived there with her daughter, who was a teenager – Lady Cecilia Fitzroy. Fitzroy was their family name and I think it was a relative of hers then was the Speaker in the House of Commons at the time.

Everybody was up by six. I had to do everything – vegetables, cleaning. As a kitchen maid, you were a skivvy, that's all you were, the lowest of the low. When I think of it now, I wonder how I ever done it. The pantry, as they called it, was as big as this room, with huge pieces of venison in, and pheasants and ducks. I would be feathering these pheasants and all the maggots would be falling out. They had to be hung so long for them to be high, before they'd eat them. On Sunday we did what we did on every other day.

Altogether four of the women worked in large private houses, starting at the bottom as scullery maids.

MIRIAM

I was working in a private house; I think they were from Bristol. One of the daughters married a factory owner in Kidderminster. He had a lot of factories up there. We had a chauffeur, a cook, a kitchen maid, then there was me and the parlour maid and the gardener.

HAZEL

We had a lady's maid, a head parlour maid, Coleman, and an under parlour maid. (Actually it was my school friend who came and had that job.) You had two house maids: the head house maid and the under house maid. You had the cook, Mrs London and a chauffeur. There was a nanny, but the children had grown – the two boys were at Oxford and Miss Elizabeth was in a finishing school in Switzerland. If there was extra sewing to be done, nanny used to come over to do the sewing. It really was *Upstairs, Downstairs*.

We had companionship, but I was so young; I was a little girl to be seen and not heard, more or less. I knew nothing about life whatsoever.

Hazel was at great pains to point out the difference between domestic and private service, the latter being superior:

I was now working for aristocracy. There was that difference. Even the young policeman looked up to you, believe it or not. It was extraordinary.

ELIZABETH

Another girl of about the same age was engaged as a house maid, so we were in the same boat. I was cleaning vegetables for the most part and washing up after cook, who seemed to use an awful lot of utensils. I didn't then know luncheon from dinner, but was soon in the picture. The rest of the staff, including the footman and butler, were also catered for in the kitchen area. Imagine my confusion on being told to lay the table for staff lunch. I hadn't a clue!

Others worked in large houses that were not quite so grand.

DOROTHY

There were four staff and I did all the dirty work; there was nobody else there to help me out. There was a huge hall and staircase: sixty-seven stairs, spiral wooden stairs, which I had to scrub once a month, the whole lot of them. The first morning I came down these stairs to the hall and I went into a little room to get a bucket of coal, because I had to have the oven hot. The cook would start frying the bacon so the oven had to be hot by half-past seven.

Then I had to rush back to the kitchen, for the cook, to cut the bacon edge for the breakfast. Then I had to lay the staff table for the cook, my aunty Flo and myself and the butler. I had to lay breakfast. As soon as we finished I had to clear all the table, wash the dishes and the ones that came down from upstairs. I didn't do their silver – it went into the pantry – but I did all the china dishes. I had to tidy up the very big kitchen, best I could.

Four of the ladies were the sole servant in their respective houses. Three of these four had come from very large families and had already experienced heavy work at home. But Eunice, being the youngest in a family of four, was quite inexperienced and yet at fourteen years old, without any formal training, she was expected to cook, clean and do the laundry for a married couple.

Kitchen duties were particularly irksome, especially the cleaning of game. Plucking and cleaning the maggoty pheasants remained one of Ceinwen's most repulsive memories. Mary W. recalls her hands being 'blood red and cracked' from washing dishes in soda. When I pressed her on what her duties had been, she said:

Washing up all the dishes, preparing all the vegetables and keeping this stove going and all that sort of thing. Plucking pheasants and chickens; skinning rabbits and hares. It was awful.

Annie remembered the poultry in her first job:

It was the same in Dr Gray's. They used to send chickens over from Ireland with the innards in because apparently they used to keep longer. It wasn't very pleasant just to take the innards out. I would have to pluck and dress the chickens, before they were cooked.

As Mrs Beeton had written a hundred years earlier, the scullery maid's first duty, at six thirty in the morning was to light the fire, to heat the oven ready for breakfast and the water for the baths. But poor Dorothy got the shock of her life the first morning she entered the kitchen early.

I opened the kitchen door and I nearly died. It was black with beetles. Black beetles. So I shut the door quick. I waited outside for about five minutes then I opened the door and peeped in again, and they had nearly all scampered away. So I waited a little bit more until I opened the door and they had all cleared off. Then I went in.

I saw those black beetles every morning, and every morning I would open the door a bit, put the lights on and stay about five minutes. Once the lights were on they were scrambling in their hundreds. There was a stove, a big sort of hot plate that I would keep the pots hot on. It was all heated and it seemed that they were scampering underneath there.

I had the job of trying to get rid of them every night. I had pieces of cardboard and I had to put stuff in the beetle tins. I had to cut cardboard and spread this stuff on them and lay those down all over the floor. They didn't seem to get any less. Then I had to sweep all those up in the morning and empty the beetle tins. I had all the job of doing all that. Mother never had anything around our house like that. I had never seen anything like that.

Other early morning routines are well remembered by some of the other women.

MIRIAM

A chambermaid is all in the bedrooms. You wake them up in the morning with their early morning tea. They all had a little tea set, one cup, one little teapot and all that. You do all the trays over night, then you make up the tea. I used to wake them up with tea and biscuits. The old lady I worked for was eighty odd, I think.

ANNIE

Madam and Sir had to have breakfast before us. I laid a tray, and the house-surgery maid took their breakfast up to bed to them. We did so many chores. I had to light the fires, to get the oven hot ready to cook. Afterwards we had our breakfast.

HAZEL

I got up at six. We had a little pot-bellied stove which kept quite hot with coke. I had to clean it out because it took all the waste disposal, all the peelings, the waste, and you had to burn that. Even in those days you could only put certain things out. I also had to go into a room, a cellar room, where all the central heating was by oil. I used to have to work this pump so that the water would be hot for them. We were only allowed one bath a week. Down one side of the room was all the best china, because Lady Cohen became lady-in-waiting to the Queen Mother. She had to go on duty at regular times.

Scrubbing the front steps was a ritual which had to be observed early each morning, come snow, rain or smog, before the master left the house. This was part of the remit for six of the women. One even had to scrub the marble statues in the Junior Carlton Club, where she worked, in addition to the front steps.

A servant's duties were considerably lighter when hot water was on tap, night or day.

(Advertising Archives)

MAY

We got up at half-past four in the morning. I was a house maid and we scrubbed on bare marble. It isn't any wonder I've got arthritis in the knees. Outside onto Pall Mall there used to be steps. I can see them now, and they had to be scrubbed and then stoned. At that time there was a lot of smog around. But whether you could see it or not, it had to be done. The footmen would come and examine those steps. They never used your name. It was 'Taff' this and 'Taff' that!

HAZEL

We had quite a big hallway which I had to keep clean. By seven o'clock, I had to go up the steps, out the front. I hated it, the only part I hated. I had to polish the big front door and scrub the front steps in the bitter cold weather even. Whether it poured or snowed, you still went out and did that.

PHYLLIS

This old lady took me on; she was crippled with arthritis. I had to do nearly everything there. The usual things, like house work, but with no modern facilities at all. Every morning, at about half-past six, I would do the porch and the front on my hands and knees – all outside. Every morning, the troops used to march up the street. At that age, you fancy those smart soldiers, so I'd be embarrassed scrubbing outside the front.

MEGAN

My job was to be up at six o'clock and I had to clean all these steps out the front, whitening them down. I think there must have been twenty and it was cold and bleak. I had to do them, not a mark had to be on them. I had to go in the back door then so as not to tread on them.

DOROTHY

There were the front steps every morning too, well, as soon as I got the fires going and built up. I had to get the buckets then and go upstairs and scrub the front steps. They were very wide and I had to get them done before the master came out of the front door. There was one big step at the top, then a little platform then about eight steps down there.

EUNICE

I used to scrub the front step and there was a little pathway that was washed down with the washing water, every week. You always washed your pavement, once a week, and scrubbed your window sills. Not like today. It's amazing, the change. I don't know whether it was for the best or not. Even after the boys married, I washed my pavement down and scrubbed the window sill. You painted window sills, so that you could keep them nice and clean.

That first day must have been an ordeal, working for strange people, far away from home.

EILEEN

Seven o'clock the following morning I had to be dressed in this uniform and come down. The daughter of the house came down to show me a coal range at the side of what they called a donkey, which heated water. That had to be cleaned out of all the ashes and lit. I had to hurry from there then into what they called the smoke room, where the captain, the master of the house, used to smoke. I remember it used to smell so heavy and I had to open these wooden shutters. I had to clean the room and I had to light a fire in there and then I had to hurry back to the kitchen to make breakfast for the other girl, Beatrice, and me.

MARGARET D.

My first job after Lapswood was in Chiswick. I went up there with this friend of mine, Vera. She was the parlour maid and I was the cook and there was a nanny there. One little boy they had. It wasn't a big house. We were there for a while.

We slept together in a small room upstairs. It wasn't a big

house, but the doctor had his main surgery down in Chiswick High Road, but the private surgery, morning and evening was at home. Vera had to look after the surgery. But when Nancy came instead of her, I went as parlour maid and had to see to the bells and things. Nance took over the cooking when we switched over.

MEGAN

My aunt was the cook general and they had a house parlour maid and I was the in-between. The first job they gave me was washing stockings, pure silk stockings, with a seam up the back. We never arrived there until four o'clock. We were given a cup of tea and I was given these stockings to wash. One of the ladies of the house was a drug addict, I never seen her; I think she was always dressed up in lace and she was in bed. The other was in the Red Cross; then there was the housekeeper and this one did a bit of everything even – golfing. I had to clean the muck off her shoes and polish them, and I had to wash and iron all her stockings. Well, the first pair I put the iron through! Oh, my aunty nearly had forty fits! So they explained how I had to put the iron on the top, the hob. I ironed them very gently, so I mastered that very well.

Some posts were more congenial than others, often simply because the employers were kind people but how many of us today would know what to do with *a polishing iron?*

DOROTHY

My favourite situation was with the Llewellyns, my last job before I married was with Dr Anderson. There was another girl, Violet, as there were two little children, and she used to take them out in the afternoons. We both wore white aprons and blue frocks. The doctor wore stiff neck collars, with the fronts. I had to do the polishing iron. Violet never used to do anything. It was always 'Dorothy, would you do it, you do it so much better then Violet.' The result then was Violet didn't have to iron the blue frocks or the children's lacy petticoats. It ended up I did all the blinking washing; I did all the ironing; and then I had to do all the polishing of his shirts. You can be too good at a thing.

EUNICE

I came home but I still had to go into service, in Dr Arwen Evans's house, in Cathedral Road. That was three floors. It was only me and a nanny. She obviously didn't do a lot of housework so I had three floors and again I had to be up at half-past six. You did everything: washing, ironing, the lot. It was rather a lot for a young, very young girl to do. But you did it, it came automatically. You didn't take any notice of it.

I had to call her 'madam' and him 'sir', but he was a real gentleman. He really was. He had patients coming to the house, private patients. We had to let them in, which meant extra dirt because he had a room for examinations and a room for patients to sit in and that was everyday except Saturday and Sunday. So whatever you were doing you had to down tools and go and answer the door all the time. Whatever you were doing!

ANNIE

I didn't want to go to London, but I didn't have a choice really. Anyway the job came up in Cardiff, so that's where I went, to Dr Gray. They were very, very, very nice people to work for. They were really nice, but it was very hard, very hard.

MARY K.

I did all the house work and the washing. One January, they said, 'It's washing day.' Out the back, with the tub. This Jack had a stall in the market and I had to scrub his coat. They took a snap of me. I had a mop of curls then. I've got my hands on my hips and I'm laughing my head off. Whatever was I laughing at I'll never know.

Jack used to tease me. He was lovely mind. He used to bring

me a box of chocolates. They used to call me 'Jo' because of my cap of many colours, like Joseph in the Bible.

Once the girls could be trusted some of their employers asked them to look after their children, and taking the baby for a walk was a relief from the day-to-day housework, something they enjoyed.

EILEEN

David must have been about six or seven months old when Mrs Balfour came to me and said, 'Eileen, I'd like to look after the children myself. Will you help me?' I thought this was wonderful. The nanny wasn't a very nice girl and because really they were getting a bit short of money, she had to go. 'I'll get someone in to help with the cleaning, because,' she said, 'I'd like you take Marianne up to the park each morning.'

Everything had to be done very carefully for these children. I had to put the cups and everything in cold water, and I brought them to the boil to sterilize them. I had to do all the nappies and hang them out. I was rushing around like mad. I was seventeen at the time, going on eighteen. I had made friends with the butcher, who used to deliver the meat – Maurice, Maurice Richardson.

Well, in the afternoon I used to take the children and the little baby as well afterwards, up to the park, and come back. They used to have a sleep while I rushed and laid the table for their lunch. The cook was there, cooking the meal. Then, in the summer, in the afternoons, the doctor had permission to use the beach at Osborne House in the fine weather. He had a new car and I used to sit in a little dickey seat at the back. The two children would be in the front. She used to drive; she had a special thing that she could use with her hand, because she couldn't use the leg. I had to be with her for lifting the children in and out. We used to be there for an hour. There would be the other elite of Cowes there, with their nannies and their children.

We'd come back, and after I had got the children to bed

there was the ironing. Everything like that was done then. I worked really hard. I mean I never finished until half-past ten at night. But as I said they never spoke unkindly. The doctor's parents were titled people. He was what I would call a real gentleman. I stayed with them until I was twenty.

PHYLLIS

On fine days she'd say, 'You leave the work and take the baby out.' I had to wear the complete nurse's uniform.

They provided it: stiff collar and cuffs, a long striped dress and apron; and two hoods, a white one and a navy one. I had a photograph taken in it, two actually. They kept one; she kept it on the baby grand piano. That was the only photograph she had. My brother pinched mine and he never gave it back. I've never been able to get it. He died.

When it came late afternoon, I would bring the baby back for lunch. Sometimes I had to stay in and she'd want such and such a room done. If not she would tell me to go back out and I would take the baby until teatime. Then she would give me work to do in the evening, like help with the cooking. The work there was ordinary cleaning and polishing. There wasn't so much furniture there. I was there for a while and they got pretty fond of me. I liked them.

EUNICE

I had to do all the ironing and, in Dr Arwen Evans' house, you know, it was a clean shirt twice a day. The nanny did the baby's clothes. On her half day I had to take Elizabeth out, up to Llandaff Fields. Nanny saw to the child and her room and the child's clothes so that was some help.

When Hilda became head parlour maid, the dining room was her province. She learnt to carve the joint and to serve champagne properly. She also became responsible for arranging the flowers, a task at which she became expert and loved doing. She also explained:

I think a month went by and then Miss Heron, the daughter said, 'Hilda, I must congratulate you on keeping the silver in good condition.' We had to clean the silver with our hands and Goddard's Plate Powder; then used brushes to get it out of the crevices and then leathers. The sink was all lead so that you wouldn't scratch anything. The glasses were beautiful. They had their crest on the silver. What a contrast to my first job!

We forget with so much radio, television and mobile phones how lonely and depressing silence can be.

EUNICE

When I was fourteen I was sent up to Melksham in Wilshire, and I had nobody. On my half day, on a Wednesday, I used to go either to the park or the pictures. On 5s a week, you couldn't go to the pictures often. You started your half day after lunch, after you had washed up and laid the trolley for tea. You had to be back by ten. You were up at half-past six; cleaned the dining room and lit the fire. Then you cleaned the sitting room fire and laid it. Laid the breakfast; went up and called the people and ran their baths. Then you came down and cooked the breakfast and had your own.

Those who worked in institutions had a different regime and the advantage of always having company.

NANCY

I was a house maid so my job was mainly the bedrooms. The nurses did their own patients' bedrooms so that my duties, when I first went there, were to do the top floor which was seven rooms, mainly staff rooms. Within a few months the first house maid left so I was promoted, not for any more money, but I was promoted. I did the bedrooms on the first floor then I waited at table. It took me all morning to do the bedrooms and I did the front staircase too.

The two house maids did the washing up, after lunch,

always, but not after breakfast; the kitchen maid did it after breakfast. We had to do it after lunch and the tea things too. Those were my responsibilities and when I first went there the reception room was my province too. That had to be done before breakfast in the morning and the fire laid there. When I was promoted, the dining room was my concern.

NELLIE
One thing we had to do was to get the *South Wales Argus* and make sticks out of it. They were lovely and you could light the fire with them. They were good.

We were ward maids. We kept the fires going, washed up, and didn't have a lot of scrubbing to do. There were other people in to do the washing; other people to do the cooking. I was just cleaning the ward, cleaning silver etc. Then there were weekends. You'd get one day off a week, and maybe one evening off a week.

More than sixty years later Phyllis has total recall of her time spent working in a gentleman's club in London.

There was a housekeeper, Kate. She was a very big, well built, tall, with a big bust, a long pink overall and a big white apron. I shall always remember the couple of big warts on her nose and her hair in that three wave style. She was very strict. Then there was the linen keeper and the staff cook. I can't remember exactly how many staff, but I know that there were six of us housemaids to a room. Over in the club were the waiters and all the chefs and everything for the businessmen. They were on their own.

About half-past five, every morning, the porter would switch on the bedroom lights and say, 'Come on girls! It's time to get up.' So we would have to get up and go down a lot of stairs to the kitchen. Very often there would be few rats there, a family of rats who used to come out in the night time because of the waste, the rubbish that was put under the sink.

We weren't scared when they come around because we were so used to them.

After a cup of tea and a biscuit, we had to go across to the basement of the club where Kate would be waiting and watching, and into the big smoking lounge and the big billiard room. There was a carpet in the middle, all surrounded by white cork lino, and the old-fashioned, big, round, iron fireplaces and the hearth.

You had to get your mop and galvanised pail and take up your dusters and the things for the fire. We had to empty the fireplaces, that was our first job, clean it all out completely. Then we couldn't just stuff paper in any how. We had to fold each piece of paper into a cone and lay it neatly in the fireplace and Kate would be there watching and her eyes would go through you. Then we had to lay small sticks down crisscross, as though you were setting a table! But the coal was left to the waiters.

Then we'd have to do all this cork lino. It was hard, because you had to scrub all that. We'd go back down for breakfast about half-past eight, then we had to go back up to the bedrooms. There was this spiral staircase, imagine, the staircase that was going up to the top floor. You had to take your galvanised bucket, your polishing cloth for your polish, soft hand brush, hard hand brush, a long sweeping brush, feather brush and a brush with a very long handle to get up in the corners and your dusters. You had to carry those right up to the top, then your first job was to check your beds, to see how many had been used. Sometimes it would be just a few. Sometimes it would be twelve that had to be changed. Every bed had a satin, gold bedspread. You daren't have a crease.

If every bed had been used, you had to go all the way back down those stairs to the linen cupboard; tell the lady in charge there what you wanted and then you had to carry that pile all the way up again. There was this young girl from Newport, Frances, and myself, round about the same age; we didn't know the dodges. The other ones were older, because they were always finished before us.

We'd have to do all that then, remake all the beds, put the satin covers on, making sure that there were no double creases or there would be a row. Fill the water jug, empty the bedpan and that. Then there were bathrooms on the landing as well which had to be scrubbed down. The floors were like a shiny grey lino that had to be scrubbed. You had to get all that done.

At half-past twelve, you'd go down for an hour for lunch, across the road again. Come back down after lunch then up those stairs again. Then you had all the rest to

Looking the part. The uniform itself was often a source of great pride.

(Catrin Stevens)

do. All the bathrooms; we had to use soda to clean them. Then it was the corridors. They did have vacuum cleaners, but all the lino had to be polished. Frances and I, we were always the two last. We were silly and we didn't dodge any corners. We'd have the landlady shouting on the stairs, 'Haven't you finished yet? You know what time it is! I want to go. I want to finish.' She'd be shouting on the stairs to us.

Then our last job was coming down the stairs to the hall. It was all wrought iron, the banisters and that. We had to clean all of them with a feather duster. Kate would be there, watching us the whole time. When we would eventually finish, it would be about half-past four to five o'clock. Then we could go and have tea.

Every night, we had to go back up about seven o'clock to draw the curtains, make sure that nobody had been there in the afternoons, put fresh water in the water bottles and a clean glass, and see if the chamber pot had been used. You'd have to turn the bed back then, take off the satin bedspread first, in its creases, lay it on the chair; turn down the corner of the sheets to match. Take the man's pyjamas and lay them neatly out and draw the curtains and then toddle off back down the stairs again, back to our quarters.

DORIS

There were hundreds of pupils at the school. It was a big place. They used to wear boater hats. In the mornings I would be cleaning the dormitories and things like that. I'd have to change clothes lunchtime and wait on tables. I expect I used to have an hour off in the afternoons. I'm not quite sure what I did in the afternoons. Then in the evenings I'd be waiting on table for the evening meal. I had to wait on sixteen girls, with one teacher at the head. It was always the same table, but not always the same girls. Sometimes they would shift around. The food was very good there. There was always a choice of menu.

The pupils were alright. You did get one or two that were a bit hoity-toity, snobbish, but the majority, they were very, very, friendly. Some of them were the same age as me. The ages varied from the little ones up to about eighteen. The highest girls had a top table, where they sat with the head of the school. They were the top, top ones. In the evenings after the meal, I used to go hair brushing. They all got to know you, because you used to brush their hair. They would say, 'We don't want to be long tonight.' Most of them had long hair. Lots of them had it done in plaits, long, long. You had to brush all that.

Interestingly Megan found also work in Malvern, but she was employed in a boys' college:

My life became harder for me on the first of May, after I turned fourteen and went to Malvern. I dearly wanted to become a cook, but I was given this job at a boys' college where my mother's sister was in the dining room. I never had any experience of learning to cook; all I seen was saucepans. My whole time (it was temporary anyhow) I had to wash up. I think there must have been sixty boys and then there was all the staff.

I had to get up and put the kettles on, on this great big range and make tea for the girls and the butler and so forth. Then they would have tea and biscuits and then I would start work, cleaning vegetables, by hand. There was no machines. My hand used to be sore, like a butcher's block. I used to have a terrible life, but I never went into the kitchen. I wasn't taught how to cook anything. I used to think, if I could only stand there and help, you know.

You had to take all the curtains down and clean all the brass rods. Clean them and wash them and put them back up. You had to scrub all the floors; beds had to be all taken out and beaten and brushed. We had a great big needle: the mattresses had like little patches on and you had to get this great big needle and string and put a new patch on each corner, for them not to wear out. We had all them jobs to do on top of doing our own jobs. When it was laundry day we had to get a big bag and put all this laundry in for the people to fetch, including the ticks, what they used to call, to cover the beds in. I remember my friend swinging it out from this door and she hit the blessed table on top of the landing. There was a pot on it and she broke it. They stopped it out of her money. She had to pay for it.

The hours were long and usually they only had one half day off a week and some Sundays. They were only allowed to go out on their half day after they had washed the lunch dishes and laid up the tea trolley. On their return, at ten o'clock, they would be expected to clean up the kitchen before they went to bed.

They did value the opportunity to learn new skills and some looked upon their time in service as an education in itself. I was told by a lady from London that girls from the East End deliberately sought jobs as domestic servants so that they could learn to speak properly. Once they had had the corners knocked off then they could get a job as a shop girl, which was considered to be better than being in service. It was arguable whether they would be any better off financially as servants had the benefit of board and lodgings.

EUNICE

They used to entertain quite a bit. Bridge parties, afternoon teas and evening dinners and things like that. The lady of the house did help if they had a dinner party, with preparations beforehand. But on the night I just had to do it and wait on table. She did show me how to lay the table, but I had an inkling of it anyway. Although we weren't very well off, my mother was proper. We'd have the side plates. We didn't have a lot of cutlery, but had the proper cutlery, with the spoon and fork.

HAZEL

I cleaned all the vegetables. Also, by now, after a few months, Mrs London was teaching me how to make sauces. I was allowed to help cook the breakfast. I was allowed to help make the cakes. You were learning, because she was teaching me now to become a cook. I did learn quite a lot.

PHYLLIS

I did everything there. It wasn't dirty work, but it was hard work. My mistress wanted me to do her blackberry pies or blackberry and apple pies. She'd tell me what to do and I would have to do it. We were alright there. You would get into the work and it doesn't seem so hard, the more you do of it.

HILDA

Mind, every morning we spent cleaning the silver and brass; that was our work mostly – and the most beautiful silver dishes and candelabra. I loved using these beautiful things –

Venetian glasses. I was responsible then for the wine and the wine cellar. I had to decant. I had the keys. They would tell you what wines they wanted, in the morning. Some wines you had to keep in the room to have the right temperatures. There was a lot to learn.

The head parlour maid taught me all these things. There had been a butler before. He retired and she took over temporarily. The cook was retiring too so the head parlour maid took over the cooking, so I was taught by her. The butler had passed on his knowledge to her; it was quite a lot to learn really. I was frightened the first time I opened champagne. The cork shot up to the ceiling! I had some frightful looks from Miss Heron. It was disgusting, but you learn. I got to wiggle it around a bit, then gradually take it out. I'll never forget that.

It was unusual for there to be any labour saving devices in the homes where the girls worked. Occasionally they were lucky.

EUNICE
They had a washing machine, an old-fashioned one. One of those that went fumph, fumph, fumph, with a thing in the middle and it had an electric roller. They had a washing machine in Melksham too. I can't remember a vacuum cleaner though. When we wanted to clean the carpet properly it was with a brush, water and disinfectant. Oh yes, you had to get down.

More often all the work was done by hand and they had to rely on 'elbow grease' alone as the labour was cheap.

MAY
We had to have a break during the day. After two o'clock, the housekeeper, Miss Evans, used to insist that we go to bed for the afternoon. We got up then and started washing up after dinner. No dishwashers as it is today. Everything had to be manual.

PHYLLIS

I had a small little room in the milliner's house, a very small room. You couldn't call it a room, with a single bed; nothing much in furniture or anything. In that place you had to do all the work. It had to be done properly. I had to do everything by hand, all the washing and all the cleaning. They didn't have a vacuum cleaner or washing machine, nothing like that.

ANNIE

I did all the rough stuff, but then on Monday it was washing day. We had to scrub the clothes on a rubbing board. Firstly I had to light the fire under the boiler, to get it hot. Then I had to scrub the clothes on the rubbing board, with a scrubbing brush, especially the whites and the collars. The linen wasn't so difficult to wash; then you had to rinse them. The whites had to be boiled, rinsed, blued, starched and then damped and rolled down to be ironed. We wouldn't get a crease in them; you had to do it absolutely properly.

HILDA

There were no vacuum cleaners in those days, only a dust pan and brush.

DOROTHY

I had to roll the coconut matting up, and you know how the dirt gets underneath that, and sweep it all out. And no electric cleaners! All brushing and then I had to whiten all the sides, wash it and whiten it. Once a week I had to do all that. Once a week I had to scrub down the seventy-six wooden spiral stairs that went to my bedroom. I had to keep the kitchen tidy and the scullery tidy. The boot hall, where they used to keep the coal, I had to do that out.

Endless toil and relentless drudgery, day in and day out, would be hard for anyone and it certainly was not a conducive occupation for a teenager.

EUNICE

I had to do all the polishing, the silver and brasses. Any spare minute you had, you'd be busy all the time. You couldn't sit down and relax. If you sat at the kitchen table there was the silver or the brasses. Something to be doing all the time. It was a very busy life really. Fortunately I didn't have to do any shopping, that was all delivered in those days. Being young, I don't know that I would have liked to have had money to look after. I don't think I'd have made a mistake, but we had been brought up very strictly. Dealing with the tradesmen might have been difficult.

PHYLLIS

It was a big house: four bedrooms, downstairs – the dining room, sitting room and the kitchen. That was my job to keep all that clean.

There were no other servants, just the one and I was that servant! My sister came back home and there I was, fourteen and a half, having to do this work. They were Jews, but they were quite nice. I had to do a room each day. Evidently this was the usual thing, wherever you went – turn out a room each day. I did that for quite a while; I got on alright with them. They were quite nice to me.

EILEEN

I worked hard there. It was a three-storey house and, of course, had open fires so I had to carry buckets of coal up to the nursery. But they were nice, nice people; good food; I had 12/6 a week. I worked still from half-past six till half-past ten at night.

Chapter 7

Working Conditions

ONE WOULD ASSUME that if a family could afford a live-in maid then they would have the space for the girl to have a bedroom. The deal was bed, board and a wage. This was not always the case as some found out to their cost. Poor Mary K., who had been too afraid to speak to her employer at Paddington after a distressing journey from Wales, finally found herself in the home of a Jewish greengrocer in the East End.

> Goodness me! I got ready now, he introduced me to them all in there and all their friends. I was scared stiff really. Then I didn't even have a bed! They take me upstairs to a lounge, a sitting room. They had these horsehair suites – my mother-in-law had one – a sofa and those chairs. That was my bed. No bedroom. I could hear the police whistles, right down by Shadwell Docks. I didn't know, coming from the country, you didn't know anything really. I didn't know where I was. I never wrote home and said I had no bed. I can't go saying anything at all. I'll just have to be mum.

I was really shocked when Phyllis just let it slip, as if it was of no importance, such a common occurrence, that she slept on a camp bed in the kitchen:

> I used to walk in the fine weather, mostly down to the Tower, around Tower Bridge; we used to go and meet up with other

The Maids' bedroom at Llanerchaeron, in stark contrast to the camp bed in the kitchen

(National Trust)

Welsh girls and other servants. It was a place for them to go, so you made friends that way. I was quite happy actually, I slept on a camp bed in the kitchen; that was my sleeping quarters.

Megan wrote down her memories and included the experiences of her friends too.

Then I had another friend, who went to Combe Martin to work, on a temporary job again, summer season. I always remember her getting fed up and she came back one Sunday. She packed her case and come home and left them. She said, 'I couldn't stand it,' She said. The mother and father, they only had a small house, they were starting up. 'I had to sleep in a shed in the garden.' Of course it was warm, because it was summer.

Some employers did not appear to see these girls as real people so any old space would suffice. Winifred Foley in her charming book *A Child of the Forest* tells of her time in service, much of which mirrors the experiences of the Welsh women.

> I had heard too much about being in service from my aunties to expect much in the way of sleeping quarters. My room seemed a novelty just the same. It was the home of the family junk; travelling bags and hobby kits, dressmaking dummies and the spades and buckets of seaside holidays. In places the junk was stacked to the ceiling, but space was left for a little iron bedstead and a small marble-topped washstand. There was a row of hooks behind the door for hanging clothes.[9]

Usually if there was more than one servant then they shared a bedroom. If they had shared a bed with several siblings at home then this was no hardship. In some cases they had their own room, which could make their loneliness more acute.

> EUNICE
> It wasn't so lonely in Cathedral Road because Molly the nanny was there. You had somebody in the evenings. In Melksham it was dreadful. Absolutely dreadful! I had a nice bedroom though. My mistress had very kindly put some books on the mantelpiece, the 'Jalna' series. She had put those there for me to read, if I had had the time!

In institutions they lived in dormitories.

> MEGAN
> We slept right up in the top of the building, the attic part. We had our own bathroom and toilet and that; and a sitting room and we walked down some steps and it was like a veranda on the top of the roof that we slept in. Six of us used to sleep in the there. We each had our own bed and chest of drawers. I walked

---

[9] Winifred Foley, *A Child in the Forest*, BBC London 1976

across and this great big rat run across the landing. Oh! My word! I jumped up on top of the chair. I always think about it. So anyway we went and told the matron and she told us, 'Rubbish, rubbish.' 'It's gone behind there,' I said. It jumped out and frightened her. From then, she rung the people and said, 'It's a big thing and it looks as if it's got a family.' I was afraid to go to sleep in the night. But nobody done nothing about it.

MAY

There were quite a lot of staff and we slept right at the very, very top of the building. There were about ten of us in the one room. There were no curtains or anything. It was just beds all over the place. There were two there from Penrhiwceiber and there was myself and another two from the Rhondda.

We used to have lots of fun in the dormitory, in our own way. There's one advantage about speaking Welsh, you see. I wouldn't do it now. But if they spoke about us, we used to speak about them too. That used to get them wild. There were more pillow fights going on when that started and quite a lot of ill feeling too.

HILDA

I didn't have to share a bedroom with my cousin; we had a bedroom each. The facilities were beautiful, lovely house, but I was sorry that I ever went there. I think I was paid three pound a month. I was young and inexperienced. I knew how to work. I knew how to clean, because we had to do that at home. There was no waiting at table because I was only house parlour maid. It was only a small house.

Even though the maids were often responsible for keeping the fires going for their employers, lighting them and fetching the coal, their own bedrooms were cold.

MIRIAM

Six staff. It wasn't that big a house, but it was big enough. It was three storey but oh! when you think of all the houses now, it was cold there; no central heating. We were up in the top floor. I shared a bedroom with the parlour maid.

MARY W.

My bedroom was over the stables in the yard. It was very cold there.

HAZEL

As good as that household was, and they were good to us with food, you could not stay in on your day off, even in the bitterest of cold weather. You had to go out. The times I've walked those streets of London without a penny in my pocket.

I don't know why they made us leave the house. I think really they would have had to feed us. When I came in, I wasn't allowed to stay up. It wasn't just me, the parlour maid; no one. I was allowed to have a hot water bottle, but although I worked in the kitchen I wasn't allowed to make myself a hot drink before I went to bed.

There was a little closet where the lady's maid used to help Miss Elizabeth to dress and everything, because they were actually washed, dressed, everything. She used to do the washing of the underwear there and we were allowed the hot water from there to take it to our bedrooms to wash. We had linoleum on the floor and a tiny little mat, just the bare necessities in that room. There was one toilet, but we didn't use it; we used the chamber pot. We'd have to empty that quickly before we went downstairs in the morning.

The word 'miserly' springs to mind when you read some of the testimonies. In spite of the fact that Hilda's mistress was a very wealthy widow owning a number of large properties, she refused to pay Hilda a reasonable rate for the job. It almost appears as if by paying them as little as possible it kept the servant in her place.

HILDA

There was a cook and a kitchen maid, head house maid, head parlour maid and under parlour maid. The lady of the house said I was a little old for an under, because I must have been twenty. I must have been because I was home for a year. She couldn't pay me as much as she would like to because she was saving for a lawn mower! Yes, that's true! She owned houses, she owned Glover's Wood. She had a house in Devereaux Gardens; she was a very rich woman: her two daughters were presented at Court.

MEGAN

My aunty was only allowed six buckets of coal a day, small buckets at that. She used to do all the cooking and everything and the heating. There were just the four of us and we used to sit at the fire in the evening. We did have a sitting room, underground, but it was that damp and cold and we weren't allowed a fire. We were only allowed to bath in this old great big tub with a big back on. Oh! It was horrible. So anyway that was a terrible place to work. We had to stand on a Friday morning, and we were given out four little pieces of emery cloth, a cup of Vim, and half a pound of soap and that had to do all the work. They wouldn't allow you to have a scrap more. It was all doled out.

Although the women I interviewed came from poor homes, some were quite well fed because their fathers cultivated allotments, so when Eileen, whose father kept chickens, had to share one egg with another servant she was very angry.

Every evening, they told us what was for food the next day. It was one egg for Beatrice and me, which I thought was very strange because I used to have a whole egg at home, because we used to have chickens up on the common. Just one egg between us. I had to beat this egg and mix some cornflour with water and add it to the egg to make it more. We were allowed one piece of toast each. They had a big field at the side of this house with chickens. They had their own chickens. They did have an egg each!

Megan also remembered her employer's reluctance to be more generous with eggs which were not being rationed in Britain between the Wars.

> We didn't have a lot of food. My aunty was given one piece of bacon to boil and it hadn't to be more than 1/6 in money. That had to do the four of us for six mornings. One piece with a piece of bread for our breakfast. Then on a Sunday we were allowed a sausage. I always remember they kept hens, right down the bottom of their ground and we had to collect the eggs. Well, they only allowed the eggs to my aunty for cooking, so if she had to make a sponge or pudding, they used to dole them out. So luckily enough, if she had one with a double yolk, she used to hide the other egg and when it was quiet she'd boil it and she'd have a piece of bread and we'd have a sandwich, between the three of us, when we went to bed in the night. It was lucky. But no butter on it, just the bread, That's how hard life was.

In contrast Margaret D. and her friend who worked together in a doctor's house in Chiswick, nearly overdosed on eggs. They had to have them every night for supper in one form or another!

> They were very tight-fisted. And I'll tell you a tale now. Marina was parlour maid and I was cook, before she left. The mistress would come out in the morning and tell me what it was I was to do for the doctor. We would have a midday lunch and whatever the doctor was having, we were having. We didn't like the foreign stuff, we liked the Welsh cooking.
>
> Well, come to the evening meal now, she would tell me, 'When I come home from the office, the doctor and I will have . . .' and she would name the dinner she wanted. And then she said, 'I thought you and Marina would have a boiled egg.' 'Right-ho madam!' The following day now, she'd come out again and tell us what we are to have lunch time and in the evening. 'Doctor and I will have such and such. I thought you and Marina would have scrambled egg.' Another night – fried egg. Marina said, 'I'll be telling her one day. I'll be asking

her, where do she think we come from?' So there we were this morning and she said, 'Madam. When Margaret and I will go back to Wales next, we'll be blushing when we do see a chicken.' 'Why do you say that?' 'Well,' she said, 'all the eggs Margaret and I are eating here for supper!'

Their mistress was also parsimonious with any treats:

> On weekends, she'd bring a lovely, gorgeous sponge back, all fancy work over it. She was very tight with the stock in the house: it was cheaper for her to buy a fancy cake for the weekend. She would never say to Marina and I, 'Have a piece of sponge.' Marina was more fit than me, I was too timid. It was always at the back of my mind, 'Taffy was a Welshman, Taffy was a thief.' But Marina would say, 'We are not working here to be starved to death! We'll have a piece of it.' And she came now for the sponge. 'Has anybody been eating...? 'Yes,' said Marina, 'Margaret and I had a piece each.' She went out with the sponge to the dining room and we didn't see it after!

Because Hazel had been dependent on the soup kitchens at home, living in such an affluent house sometimes upset her.

> Lady Cohen used to go out to St Moritz and you would have Sir Lionel still at home. By now I was doing the cooking for him. He was extremely nice. He would come down into the kitchen and say, 'Thank you Hazel! That was very nice.' He always complimented you and on what you did. It used to break my heart when I used to clean potatoes, and you used to peel potatoes away until they were small little balls. You wasted all those potatoes.

Eileen too had a problem with potatoes and also Jerusalem artichokes, which were used as a substitute sometimes.

> The potatoes were counted so we only had one potato each. Although I was cooking, I couldn't take a bit of extra food

A soup kitchen in Treorchy, 1926. (Rhondda Cynon Taf Library Service)

for Beatrice and me because our dinner was served from the dining room. She served ours after she had served the others.

All the vegetables were grown in the grounds. I remember the potatoes: before the new potatoes came they used to go a bit short so they used artichokes and they were horrible. They were all knobbly things that had to be scrapped. I hated the taste of these artichokes. I said to Beatrice, 'Tell the mistress not to put any artichokes out for me. I can't stand them.' I suppose the girl told her and oh dear, if she did. She came out and said to me, 'How dare you! How dare you say that you don't like anything. You've got to eat what I give you.'

A clumsy girl could cost a fortune in breakages. In order to make them more responsible when accidents happened, the servant was expected to reimburse their employer for the damage caused. This would cause problems as very often the maid did not have any money for these untoward events; or to avoid paying she might be compelled to cheat her mistress and hide or destroy any such evidence. Hilda started as she meant to go on.

When I took over the parlour work, I found a lot of breakages at the back of a cupboard! I didn't know what to do, because I wasn't responsible for them. I asked if I could go through to the morning room, because Mrs Jansen was there in the mornings. It was a busy life for a person like her. There was a lot of business to attend to. She said, 'Yes?' I said, 'I have taken over the parlour work as you know, Ma'am. I find that there are quite a few breakages in the pantry cupboard.' She said, 'When I have finished writing, I'll come out and I'll see.' So I got them all out on the pantry shelves. Some of the things could be repaired because they had put things at the back that were of value. Some weren't. Those were discarded. I knew where I was then. She said, 'Thank you for telling me.' So I started off with a clean slate, didn't I?

Margaret C. was not so fortunate.

I never regretted the time I was in service, only when Mrs Ellwood left me in Fern House. I didn't like my other maid. We were washing up. We had a great big kitchen and a big scullery. I was in the kitchen, washing up, with Mabel my friend. There was a cheese dish. I don't know how it happened. I can't remember who was washing and who was wiping. We put it on the table and it slipped off and she said, 'I shall have to keep that out of your wages.' I think we were having 10s a week then. It was 17/6. We had to take it out of our wages. I was indignant because we didn't know if we had done it.

As in all walks of life there are the good and the bad, the kind and the unkind. A couple of the women experienced deliberate callousness. Eileen put the fact that her mistress was particularly spiteful down to the fact that she was not English.

He was English but she was what we used to call Cape Dutch. He was captain in the South African police and he'd married her there. She was the most horrible woman. Looking back on it now I realised that she was used to lots of black girl servants. She was treating us not like white girls. Oh it was terrible.

There was the front stairs where the family came down and there was the back stairs with no carpet on which we came down, because we shared a bedroom. I always knew by her footsteps coming down these stairs whether I was going to have a row or not, whether she was in a good mood. Never mind what you'd done, she found something wrong. It was a stone flagstone floor and I used to get in a terrible mess because it all had to be done with this red ochre.

I can remember crying one day that I wanted to go home. The daughter, Miss Maureen as she was called, I think she felt sorry for me, but out come the Madam and she said, 'You can go if you like!' I don't know what she said to me altogether, but she drummed it into me that my mother had to buy all these clothes, which made me frightened for my mother now because she had spent all this money you see.

I carried on.

Some were made to feel invisible by their employers and this was indeed how domestic service was meant to be carried out.

EUNICE
To my employers I was just a servant and that was it. I felt invisible. You'd clean and you'd find things. You'd pick up a rug and there'd be money under it. You would leave it there obviously. You wouldn't say anything. It was so silly. She could have left it hanging about anywhere, but under the rug! It was horrible really. It was degrading.

Staff were never allowed to be found on the main staircase; work had to be carried out in the family rooms early in the morning before the family came downstairs. An efficiently run house would appear as if it was run by pure magic! This did not take into account any feelings that the staff may have had sensing that they were under appreciated and becoming resentful.

Then there were the plain bone-idle mistresses as Phyllis discovered:

She was horrible and lazy and dirty. I had to do everything there. She didn't bother much with the baby that was all my responsibility. The cleaning up was my responsibility too.

She would always send me out to get a box of Neapolitan chocolates. She would sit back in the chair and she would munch, munch away at these Neapolitans. I would be carrying on with everything to do – all the washing, the baby, all the cleaning. As long as it was done, she didn't care what or when. She was even that lazy that she would have a chamber pot by the side of her, to save her going to the toilet. I was working for that.

It was not only employers that could be unkind as Dorothy discovered. The other staff could make life hard for the young maids too.

They had a room there, a sitting room for the staff. I never, once in the whole of the year I was there, went in there. Even at nine o'clock at night, perhaps if I had finished at quarter past nine, I would want to go in the room. I was told, 'Oh no, no. You go to bed. You've got to get up early in the morning. You're first up.' So I used to go upstairs to my bed and have a jolly good cry. I was never allowed in that room. I was much younger than the other staff.

Conversely both Hilda and Doris were happy with their working companions.

HILDA
It was great fun; seven of us at the table. The cook housekeeper was very strict. You had to be in at a certain time. The company was good. There was one other Welsh girl there, briefly, from Tylorstown. Some of the other girls were from Norfolk. It was the postman that recommended me because he knew me from the Red House, from the previous house. It was a lovely place. The postman was such a good friend, a lovely friend. He came to the same house, of course. He said, 'Are you happy?' 'Yes, I'm very happy.' 'I thought you would be', he said. 'It would be just your cup of tea.'

DORIS

There were lots of other girls working there. They weren't all the same age, some were older and had been there years. They came from everywhere, but they were a grand crowd of people. They were really nice.

Hilda did feel valued and was appreciative of the fact that she had landed on her feet and was working in a very fine establishment:

My second job was different. It was in the same village, but a couple of miles away from the Red House. It was called Newdigate Place. It was big manor house, with a surrounding deer park and lakes. They had gardeners and a garden boy. They had their own farm with their own gamekeeper and their own lodges – three lodges. It was a fantastic place. I've got a photograph of the house; a billiard room; their own tennis courts. We were seven staff indoors.

What a difference in the attitude towards me and the rest of the staff, to my first job. You were respected for what you did. We had a beautiful servants' hall and we each had our own particular job. As an under, I had the morning room to do and light the fire and clean. When I became head parlour maid my work altered again.

There were no men in the house. So there was a staff of seven just for the two ladies. Quite a few guests came from time to time, members of the family. During that time there was entertainment; in the summer time there were tennis parties; sherry parties as they called them in those days, garden parties. The house was full; it was seldom without company. Mr Jansen had been a wool merchant and Mrs Jansen had inherited money of her own. She was more or less like a lady of the manor. She did wonderful work. If people were ill in the village, the chauffeur was sent down with soup or something like that.

Living in someone else's home at such close quarters meant that the women were exposed to new ways of living and often completely different cultures. Jewish families usually employed a maid even if they were only working class themselves; there was so much work to be done, especially in large families. Many Welsh girls found themselves working for Jewish families in London.

MARY K.

Up the next morning, I didn't do any cooking, so I thought I would hoover. This Jack now was in the lounge, with his little hat on and he was there, 'Blah, blah, blah.' I was just going to hoover the room. I thought, 'Whatever is he doing?' The penny dropped! He was praying. I though it best to get out of the way, with this hoover into the other room.

We had the feast of the Passover. Friday was Shabbat, when we'd light the candles and I'd have to go inside and have a drop of this wine. There were different plates and we lived on matzos for a whole week. I had ulcers on my gums! The matzos! I remember going around the market and I bought a hot cross bun and what do you think happened? I got to the door and not a word was said and they grabbed me. I was whipped through, out into the garden! I didn't know what I had done. 'Whatever is the matter?' I asked. She said that I was not supposed to walk through with this bun; unleavened bread they were calling it.

Then they wouldn't strike a match. They would go to *schule*. The Jewish religion, I was intrigued with it. I thought 'Well, dear me.' They were very devout.

I had a friend in Bethnal Green, she blew all the candles out! She blew the candles out! I knew the candles were there for something, so I just thought, a prayer. She blew all the candles out, oh dear, dear! There were loads of Welsh girls down there, working for the Jews, about fifteen or sixteen of them.

They were very nice though. I was in with them having meals and I had never tasted chicken until I got there. Beautiful food, the Jewish food. They used to call me 'The Schickster'. 'The Schickster loves the food!' I thought, 'Yes, I should think so!' I liked everything they had; herring mops in wine vinegar with onions and those lovely bagels.

May, a good Methodist, met her match in the club dormitory.

There were some Roman Catholics there. Of course they were allowed Friday, to go to confession and mass. We had to do their work while they were away. The work had to go on. They wouldn't consider giving us any hours. They were allowed to have fish on a Friday, but we had to eat whatever was given us.

They used to always make fun. We were always taught to say our prayers at the side of the bed on our knees. Thank goodness I have now come to the conclusion that He will hear me wherever I am. But of course they used to be with their rosaries. That wasn't enough; they used to taunt me about 'What are you saying your prayers for Taff?' 'What do you expect to have for them?' I would say, 'I know I'll have more than you, counting your beads.' I didn't know that they were rosaries. That's the way I used to retaliate.

It was not uncommon for the employer to change the name of the employee if it was considered unsuitable for some reason. Obviously the use of nicknames was understandable, although May found being called 'Taff' by the footman offensive. Mary K.'s Jewish family often referred to her as the 'Schickster'. Ceinwen was called 'Jane' as they could not pronounce her real name and Margaret D.'s colleague was renamed 'Elizabeth', although Margaret D. always called her 'Marina'. Together they were addressed as 'you two young people.' It was the complete change of name that denied the women their own identity and no name at all denied them their very existence.

Chapter 8

Making a Life – Money and Mischief

THE FIRST EXPENSE that the maids had would be their uniform, which they had to buy themselves. The thinking behind this, was that if you had to buy every new maid her uniform then you would soon be out of pocket yourself. By paying for it themselves then it belonged to them, fitted them properly and could be worn in any job. The girls would look after it if they had actually paid for it. You do read of how footmen used to have their livery supplied, but usually the next man was chosen because he fitted the vacant coat!

CEINWEN
It was £2 a month and 10s of that had to go back to Mrs Knight (the agent) to pay for the uniform. I had half a day off a week and a half-day every other Sunday

MIRIAM
I was paid 10s a week, £2 a month. We had to buy our uniforms and our clothes and everything. I couldn't send any money home.

The next expense was the fare to the job. If the parents were unable to afford to pay it then again it would be advanced by the new employer. There was a risk in this arrangement in that the girl might be unsatisfactory and may have to be sacked, or she might not like the job and leave of her own accord before the debt was paid.

Dear Madam

nr Glynneath
Nov 17/11/39

Just a few lines to let you know madam, that I am very sorry that I cannot start today (Friday) as I havn't had all my uniform. but I hope you will not mind me coming on Saturday afternoon I am very sorry that if I have made it inconvient for you, Madam, or better still I will be down at "Baylan Hall" about 10–30 to 12 oclock.

I remain Yours
Sincerely

No uniform, no work! A maid's apology to Madam.　　(Glamorgan Archives)

DOROTHY

I went back home after a year and I had to pay my own fare; you never got any gratuity from those people, I can tell you. I think service was dreadful in those days. They used to send us home on our week of annual holiday. They didn't even pay our wages in some places. We had to pay our own fare and naturally we had to give money to keep us. Mother couldn't afford to keep us. We had to do that out of our savings.

MIRIAM

I couldn't really afford to come home for a bit. I know the fares weren't much but we had to use our money for so many things. It took me a long time to save up before I could come home, for my fortnight yearly holiday.

MAY

I was earning about seven or eight shillings and then it went up to twelve and six, and that had to come back to Mam. I kept about three or four shillings: enough to see us tidy; to get us home once a year. Then we had to pay for our keep when we came home. You couldn't be home here without paying something.

Morddfa took about six months to clear her debt which her London family had advanced for the train fare, which then had to be paid off over the weeks, by being deducted from her wages.

A very sad case was reported in the *Free Press of Monmouthshire*, dated 7 January 1927, where a girl was sacked after only a week.

> Having been found sitting disconsolately on her luggage in Greenwood Place, St Pancreas, Lucy Heynon (22), a domestic servant, of High Street, Garndiffaith, was charged at Marylebone with wandering abroad and lodging in the open air.
>
> The police stated that she told them that she had been discharged from her place of employment and had nowhere to go. She told the magistrate, Mr Bingley, that she came up from Wales to a situation in London and was given notice the following week. She had not sufficient money to return home, and was stranded.
>
> The magistrate discharged her and handed her over to the missionary.
>
> It will be recalled that the London magistrates have had cause to call the attention of the public to several cases of the kind during recent months, and to denounce the reprehensible practice of enticing girls to the Metropolis, after which they are left stranded.
>
> A local sister, who has had to deal with previous cases of the kind from the Eastern Valley of Monmouthshire, informed the 'Free Press' that the custom resorted to by some unprincipled people is to advertise situations for domestic servants 'with fare paid to London'. When the girls are dismissed shortly after taking up the situations they are told no wages are due to them inasmuch as they were expected to

work for money advance for their fare. Thus the unfortunate young women find themselves stranded in a strange city without means to return home. Disclosures of the kind should act as a warning to young girls contemplating service in large cities to make the strictest investigations before accepting the situations advertised.

This particular girl seems quite old at 22 to get into this situation, but there were a number of voluntary welfare organisations, which the magistrate had referred to as missionaries. These were aware of the difficulties in which the girls might find themselves. Sometimes middle-class matrons handed out leaflets to the young girls as they arrived at the railway stations in London to warn them of dangers and to give them a contact address in case they were in trouble. One such philanthropic volunteer society was the Metropolitan Association for the Befriending of Young Servants. Their role was to befriend young girls in service, protect them from harassment, provide safe lodgings and save them from the ultimate fear, that of being forced into prostitution by untoward circumstances.

In 1927 the same newspaper reported a meeting held in Pontypool where a Mrs Peter Hughes Griffiths, of London, spoke of her work in connection with the problem of the Welsh girls in London:

> In 1925 the London Welsh Presbytery set up a committee to deal with the matter. Last year the Bow Street magistrate drew attention to the number of Welsh girls coming up to the East End of London, and said he would be very grateful if some recognised society would help him by communicating with those girls who had no means of returning to Wales if they so desired.
>
> The Welsh Women's Temperance Union felt they ought to do something in the matter. Dame Lloyd George presided at a conference, which was attended by all the Welsh clergy and ministers in London. There were 30 Welsh Churches of all dominations there, and these were asked to send three women representatives each, together with other Welsh organisations.

The meeting was a very interesting one, and all sorts of suggestions were made.

The name of the Society that was formed was 'The London Welsh Friendly Aid Society for Girls', and since its inception they had been inundated with inquiries from parents who had lost touch with their daughters, and from girls who required guidance and help. They were fortunate in having the services of a retired police detective, who received no pay, but only out of pocket expenses. To effectively deal with the cases that came before the Society needed a great deal of tact and knowledge of human nature. One of their great problems was with girls who came up to London and were not connected with any of the churches. Those who were connected could bring transfer tickets, get in touch with others, and begin to feel at home.

Mrs Griffiths thought that girls were allowed to leave home for London at far too young an age. The society had had a great many cases of girls only 14 or 15 years of age. It would be of tremendous value if those girls during the last few years at school were given a training in domestic work.

Mrs H. H. Pratt referred to the work of the Labour Exchange at Pontypool. Everything possible was done there to ensure girls getting good situations. She also gave details of the work done in that Hall and at Griffithstown in the matter of domestic training.

Myth has it that these girls not only worked for a pittance, but they even managed to send money home. Unfortunately I only asked seventy per cent of them this question and of that number, only half did so. It is very difficult for me to give an average figure for a week's wage; what is more, it is virtually impossible to compare the value of money between now and then. Money's real value is in its purchasing power and when a loaf of bread cost 9d in 1930 and today is on average £1, we get into the confusion of old money combined with inflation. It is annoying to read that something costs 2/6 followed in brackets by the figure of 25p. In 1930 one could buy just over three loaves of bread for 2/6 (in fact three loaves would have cost only 2/3) whereas today you could only buy ¼ of a loaf for 25p. However, another good yardstick of comparison is the price of a man's tailored suit – an average suit costs an average week's wage. The average wage for these girls was about 7/6, when a suit cost 50 shillings. I have calculated that this is in the region of £45 a week, in 2010. They were also provided with their food and accommodation, as demonstrated in the previous chapter, the quality of which could vary tremendously.

EILEEN

Anyhow this 10s a week I was having: the arrangement was that I would send 5s home and keep 5s. I had to save for my fare for going home or stockings or anything I needed. Opposite the house there was a little thatched pub called The Pineapple and there was a little sweet shop along the side of it. We used to slip across and buy a few sweets. I never had anything else but that.

MEGAN

Then of course, my job was to do all the dirty work. And it was dirty work, for which I received £1 a calendar month, £12 a year. Out of that £1 I had to send 15s home, for my mother, to keep the house going and I had to send my dad a shilling for some cigarettes and 4½d to register the envelope. So out of the little bit I had left, I had to have my shoes heeled, which cost 1s and I had two pairs of stockings, 6d a pair. So that was all I had, and of course a stamp home. I never knew what it was to buy a penn'orth of toffee.

DOROTHY

I was having 30s per calendar month. I used to send a pound a month home to my mother and I kept 10s for myself.

HAZEL

Lady Cohen used to come and give the orders. Mrs London used to go to the top of the stairs and she would give the orders for the day. The only time that I saw her was when she gave me my pay, 10s of which I sent home regularly to mother every month. Considering I only had 6s a week, 24s a month, I only had 14s left to last me for a month.

PHYLLIS
I think it was a good experience, but we did work very hard and the money first started at 7/6, then it went up to 10s in another job, but the last job was 15s. You did send some home to your mother because you were earning that much more. I think a few shillings at that time meant a lot to your mother.

MARY K.
I got 7/6 a week and they expected me to send money home out of that.

MARY W.
I was paid thirty shillings a month. I used to send ten shillings home to my mother and keep the pound for myself, every month. I stayed there for two and a half years.

Those who did not send money home were expected to keep themselves in clothes and any other necessities. The rationale about these young girls having to leave home was that they were not to be a drain on their impoverished families back in Wales during these difficult economic times. They were expected to stand on their own two feet.

HAZEL
I worked from six in the morning until ten at night for 6s a week. Out of that I still had to buy my own day-to-day clothes.

EUNICE
I didn't have to send any money home. I had to buy my own clothes and for my days off I had to have my 5s a week. I had to save to come home on holidays, if I had any. Mam never did make me sent my money home. She didn't really need it by then. Of course in the big Depression she would have needed it, but I wasn't around then.

PHYLLIS

They paid me 7/6 a week. I don't remember sending it home. The only thing I can remember was, when I had my pay, the first thing was to buy the half slab of chocolate that was my luxury for the week.

NANCY

I got 7/6 a week and I wasn't expected to send any of it home. I could keep it.

ANNIE

We had one pound per month, which was quite a lot of money in those days, because that pound a month did quite a lot. I travelled on my day off to Mountain Ash and back. That pound had to last me all month. I had to keep myself in clothing out of that. It was a bit of a struggle, but Mum didn't expect anything from me, because she liked me to keep myself respectable. I had to buy myself winter clothes when necessary.

ELIZABETH

I was paid four pounds per month and sent ten shillings home to my mother, until my father told me not to.

Occasionally the girls were brave enough to negotiate a higher rate, but this did not happen often. Both Dorothy and Hazel were particularly feisty individuals and realised their own value.

DOROTHY

They'd had a girl then, she was leaving. They were paying her 21s a calendar month. But she was twenty-one. So when they said about my wages, they came down to about 15s a calendar month. I said, 'Oh no. I want the same money as the other girl was having.' 'Oh you can't have that. After all, she's twenty-one and you're only. . .' I said I was between sixteen and seventeen. I wasn't, I was just gone fifteen. He said, 'You can't do that. You're only young. She's so much older than you.'

I said, 'I'll tell you what I'll do Mr Tom,' (I called him that, the father then was Mr Llewellyn, the old man). 'What I'll do Mr Llewellyn, I'll work for the month and if you don't think that I've earned that money at the end of the month you can drop me down. But if I done it, I want the same money as she's having.' 'Fair enough,' he said, 'Alright we'll do that.' So at the end of the month he called me and said, 'Well, Dorothy, a month is up, isn't it?' I said, 'Yes, sir. What have you decided?' 'We are giving you the money. We think you are a very good worker. You shall have the same as she had.'

HAZEL

One day Coleman came down to me and she said, 'Hazel, will you go upstairs and carry Sir Lionel's suitcases down please?' I just looked at her and I said, 'Sorry, Coleman, I'm not doing it.' 'What do you mean?' she said. 'I've been here three years and I have never been allowed to be seen, and now you are asking me to carry Sir Lionel's suitcases down.' I know I said he used to come in the kitchen and always thanked me. 'Now the work is getting more and more and I'm not getting paid any more.' I flatly refused and I didn't. Lady Cohen called me to the top of the stairs and I said, 'I'm sorry your Ladyship but I'm not doing it.' So she put my money up by a shilling a week.

Life was a serious business for these women when they were girls. They were working more than fifteen hours a day and there were not many opportunities for fun or high spirits. Margaret D found a job with her friend Marina. They came from the same village and had been to Lapswood Training School together too. There would have been a boldness in their friendship due its longevity. It is not surprising therefore to learn that they got up to mischief. The very idea of leaving two fifteen-year-olds in the house all day by themselves makes one wonder at their employers' wisdom.

MARGARET D.

One day, the postman came to the door. 'That's alright, Marina. Don't come down. I'll go to the door.' The postman handed me a big box. Something for the mistress from Peter Robinson. 'She's been buying something again, I expect, isn't it.' I put it on the chair. I went on with my work now, cooking. Marina was supposed to be upstairs. She was a daring girl, terrible. The back door bell went. Nobody there! I must have imagined it. Well, after a while the front door bell went. I went to the door. Where was Marina? There was Marina, dressed up to the nines. Hat, everything. 'Oh!' I said. 'Where did you get that from?' 'Well, that's what come in the post this morning!' 'Oh, Marina!' I said. 'Go up quick in case someone comes in; in case she comes back and sees it! Oh, Marina!' I was a bath of perspiration. Sometimes things weren't too hot for me, but that was a bit much. She'd taken it out of the parcel! The hat and everything. 'Oh Marina, take it!'

The mistress come home now. 'Parcel come for me?' 'Yes.' Later on that night, she come out now, after she had had her dinner. 'Now I want you two young people to come up and see my new outfit.' I said, 'You go first, Marina, I'm not coming with you. You go first, I'm busy. I'll come up later.' 'Oh nice madam, beautiful.' But she had already seen it, you see. Oooh she was an awful daring girl. She didn't care a bit see. Nothing! She was terrible. She was beyond.

One day Marina nearly got caught!

They used to go up to the West End a lot, once a week they would go. Upstairs we would go then and try all the Madam's clothes on. Dresses, gowns, hats. Sometimes the nanny would come in and have a little joke with us. But this day when we were all dressed up, we heard the door going. They'd come back. Ooh there was a panic now honestly, there was a panic! 'Oh Duw, Duw, Marina!' 'Never mind now! Sling them in the wardrobe and pretend they had fallen off the rack,' she said.

'Sling them in quick! Sling them in!' We ran to our bedroom then, to get dressed tidy. She was an awful girl. Terrible. Nothing too hot for her to do.

Although these girls were only playing around, we forget that clothes had a real value and would be worth stealing. Wardrobes used to have a lock and key whereas today, as most people no longer have staff, they do not. We all have plenty of clothes and most are not of great value.

Mary K. too took advantage of being left in charge of the house in her employer's absence.

> She was in business all day and he was. I think one of the sons was a doctor in a hospital. I think she had two sons home and a lovely daughter. She was about twelve. She was sweet. They were off all day. We used to get on with the work. Then they went away and they left us for a weekend with the little girl, so we had a party. That was very daring, a lovely party. I had a boyfriend then from home. He came. They all came. We had a party and the little girl was there. She never let on. Oh, she was sweet, she was lovely.

Megan and her aunty paid a high price, literally, for disobeying instructions to beat the carpets, when they were left alone.

> My aunty said to me, 'Don't say anything, but when the doctor goes out tonight, that woman will come around to peep on us. They've got a vacuum cleaner. We'll vacuum it all and roll it up; they won't know we haven't beaten it on the line.'
>
> But they had locked it away. She found the key and we got the vacuum cleaner out. She said to me, 'You keep on doing it. Go up and down straight, keep doing it.' My aunty turned around and said, 'Here, you're not doing it right. Do it like this!' And the blessed vacuum cleaner gobbled up the lead. Ooh! I'll never forget it. She didn't know what to do then. We folded the carpet up and put the vacuum cleaner back. She had to phone the people to come and see it. It was a Hoover.

Bless my life, if she didn't get the man to come. And he said, 'Well, it will cost you 7/6 to have it repaired. I'll do it while I'm here.' She gave him her 7/6, out of her 10s a week. Poor aunty! He got it right and she cleaned it all and she put it back in the cupboard.

Margaret C.'s friend Vera even disobeyed the doctor.

Vera was terrible. 'Will you deliver this medicine, Vera?' the doctor would say. 'Damn!' she'd say, 'I'm not going down there. I'll phone him up and ask him to send somebody up for it.' 'Don't do that, Vera.' 'Yes. I'm not going down there. Someone in the family will come and pick it up.' Oh she was a terror at times. They were complaining to the doctor. He said, 'Deliver it! Don't ask them to come up and fetch it.' Nothing was too hot for her to do, you know.

Doris and her co-workers in the college were just as full of high spirits as any such teenagers would be in their situation, but she considered her behaviour quite daring:

I used to go out with one of the girls that worked in the same place on our half days. When it was time to come home, we used to go to the top of the mountain, 'cos we had to be in by twelve o'clock. We were on top of the mountain when the clock was striking twelve. We had to race down the mountain and we got to the side door; it was locked. The door was locked right on twelve. We had to throw a handful of stones to the girls' window. They would creep down and let us in and we would go through the passage and we'd get to the pantry. We'd dive in there and we put fruit in our pockets; apples, oranges and so forth and start down the passage. The cook would come out – 'Come back here! Come back here!' We'd say, 'Ta, ta!' And we'd be gone. 'See you in the morning!' That's what I used to get up to!

Phyllis's sister wanted her to come to work in the same place as her. So she persuaded Phillis to lie to her employer:

My sister said, 'Tell you what. I'll give you a ring about eleven o'clock. If she asks you what it is for, tell her that Mam wants you to go home.' I was very, very guilty. I didn't like doing it at all. The only good thing was that I would be more with my sister. Funny thing, that very morning I was just getting out of my camp bed, when the door opened and my Mrs was there. 'Oh Phyllis,' she said, 'You're still there.' Tears started running down her cheeks. 'I was dreaming last night that you had left me.' I felt so terrible; I didn't know what to do; I couldn't say anything to my sister in between.

The phone rang at eleven and I never answered the phone but my Mrs said, 'It's for you.' I had to make an excuse that somebody was ill back home and I had to go back home. She knew I was lying. The bad part about that was I went to work for the daughter and she was horrible.

Mary K. led a very convoluted life in and out of jobs, answering back and generally being high spirited. She would have been a hard girl to control for any mistress!

I went upstairs where I shared a bedroom with a lovely girl. I said, 'I don't think I'll be here long.' It went on and on and I'd made friends now with a girl from Leamington Road. She was a cook from Treherbert. She said to me, 'We want a parlour maid.' I said, 'Do you really? That place I've got is terrible.' She said, 'Well I'll tell you what, I've got to give my notice.' I'd been there a month. A month's wages was three pounds. If I got my three pound, I was going to run away. I said to the parlour maid, 'I'm going to tell you a secret. I'm going to run away. 'Oh. I won't say a word,' she said.

The night came and the lady came to tell me what was for breakfast. I cooked asparagus. I was a good cook. At four o'clock in the middle of the night, my friend said she would leave the window open, around the side. I came right down West End Lane in the dark. She had the back door open. I opened the window, went through the window and right up the stairs. The lady hadn't seen me even. I landed there as a parlour maid. I had forty-three jobs in a year.

One does question the value of that all important reference, because if you had forty-three jobs in one year then there would never be time for the reference to be taken up. It does also illustrate how plentiful vacancies for domestic servants must have been. Mary K.'s story continues!

But it came to a head one day. It was a Sunday, I think. I was doing the ironing and in she comes and she said to me, 'These handkerchiefs are not ironed properly. They might me good enough for your miner brothers, but they are not good enough for my gentlemen sons.' I was cross about that. I thought, 'Right you.' I went white. I let it go. The following week the basket came in; a huge basket with the laundry in it. They used to send things to the laundry; we did the little things, but not the other things. I thought, 'That's heavy.' I had to take it upstairs. I knocked the door. I said, 'Excuse me, Madam. Would you lend me your gentleman son, to help me with the laundry basket?' She looked at me. 'It's rather heavy for me.' I said, 'And Gladys is off duty.' She was the cook. She herself came to catch hold of the handle with me. Well, I got cheeky now.

What happened then was a terrible row. I was going off duty and she was having a row with the cook. It was going to be my half day; I was courting my husband then and I had arranged to meet him on the corner. I think my friend said she was going to leave, to give her notice. 'Take that pretty beauty with you!' In I go, 'Excuse me Madam. Are you referring to me? Right! I'll go now,' I said. 'Certainly! Madam. I shall pack my case now, but I'd like my month's wages, before I go. You've given me notice to go immediately with no notice. I'll certainly go.' She looked at me. I said, 'Gladys, get our case packed!'

She looked at me. There was no sign of her giving me any money, so do you know what I did? I was in my uniform and my apron. I don't know where I had the cheek from. Round the corner was the police station. I thought, 'Right!' My boyfriend was waiting for me now. I went to the police station. 'Excuse me I've got a complaint.' 'You Welsh girls are always in trouble.' 'Well really. It's a different matter now,' I said. 'I want to complain to you. I've been told to leave at a minute's notice.' 'What have you done?' 'I haven't done anything. I only want my month's wages and I'm willing to go, ' I didn't tell him I'd run away from the other place. They started to snigger. One of them said, 'Come in here, my dear.' He called me into the office. 'Now tell me now what you've done.' 'I haven't done anything. My friend is the cook and from there she was going and she had to take 'That pretty beauty' with her.' 'Tell you what,' he said. 'I'll come up with you. It's only round the corner.'

I'm walking up now, in my uniform on a Sunday afternoon, and my boy friend is at the corner. He looks up. 'Whatever has she been up to now?' We get to the door. 'Can I come in? I'm coming in to pack my case.' The policeman came in to sort things out. She took him into the dining room; I said to Gladys, 'Where on earth have you been? I've been trying to get our month's wages for us to go. She's terrible.' I saw her give the policeman money and he came out to us and said, 'I've talked it over. What I suggest you both do is to give your notice in now and work your month's notice out. Because that's the best thing you can do.' We couldn't walk out because we had nowhere to go and we had no money.

The little girl was lovely and the husband was lovely, but she was dreadful. I got dressed now and I met my boyfriend. 'Whatever have you been up to now?' 'Nothing,' I said. 'But she's been on to us terrible.' She advertised and she said, 'I'll never take Welsh girls again.' I said, 'I think you should go back to Jerusalem.' I did! I was so cross. I got cheeky.

The local press in Wales would report what was going on in the London courts if there was Welsh interest. One such account

I found in the *The Free Press of Monmouthshire*, dated 4 August 1927, had the headline 'Welsh Girls Charged in London.' It went on to describe how two young servant girls, Gladys Thomas and Hazel Johnston, employed in South Kensington, were charged at Westminster,

> with burglariously entering an adjoining house and stealing wearing apparel and a scent spray.
>
> Detective-sergeant Martin said both girls came from South Wales and had good characters. They had been in their present situations some time and their conduct was inexplicable to their mistress.
>
> Mr Boyd said there was not enough evidence to justify a charge of burglary, and he would deal with the case next week. In the meantime they would be remanded and their friends would be communicated with in order that they might go back to their homes. He did not think it desirable that they should remain in London.

Chapter 9

Time Off

ALTHOUGH IN THEORY the girls should have had regular periods of rest and time to themselves it was not always given with good grace. If you had a young girl under your roof, eating your food and you were paying her as well, albeit a pittance, then you would not want her gadding about or sitting still. There was no organised union for domestic workers to fight their corner and also they were women out of sight, many in private houses. It was not until June 1938 that the National Union of Domestic Workers was formed, under the auspices of the TUC. The membership reached a peak of 805 in June 1939 and the Union ceased its existence in May 1953.[10] These bare facts speak for themselves. There were hundreds of thousands of servants in London alone; they were probably unaware of the existence of such a union. Young girls working well into the evening are not going to spend their precious free time going to meetings to better their conditions when they saw service as an interim part of their lives, a rite of passage between school and marriage. However they usually had one half day and one whole day at the weekend if they were lucky.

MAY
During the week we had half a day off and one Sunday in six; not the whole Sunday because we had to be up to light the coal fires.

---

[10] London Metropolitan University Archive

Welsh expatriates had a tremendous network in London dating as far back as 1485. London is the home to the oldest and largest Welsh community outside Wales. From the accession of Henry Tudor the numbers of Welsh men and women living in London increased steadily. The middle of the nineteenth century saw another surge towards London. This was the age of the dairymen and drapers and the rise of the chapel as a focus for Welsh life in London. During the Depression there was another massive influx as Welsh teachers, industrial workers and domestic servants sought work in the metropolis.[11]

HAZEL

There was a Welsh Club just by the BBC studios which I used to go to when I could afford it. Also there was a Welsh Corner [in Hyde Park], still going in London today. I'd go there on a Sunday evening, before I would go home by ten.

We used to meet boys at the Welsh Club, but I was extremely shy. Muriel [her sister] could dance, but I couldn't. I had two left feet. Unless you danced, that was it. I remember having my first port and lemon. Muriel thought it was very sophisticated. One of the boys bought it and I didn't like it at all!

MARY K.

I used to go down to Hackney to find somebody. In the end we were a gang of Welsh girls. My friend said to me, 'Come up to Hyde Park.' I thought, 'How am I going to get there?' I got on the train, to the Bank. Then I got on the bus and I said to the driver, 'I want to get to Hyde Park and will you tell me when we get there?' I sat in the corner. It must have been cheap because I didn't have much money. Right! My friends said there was a run there and all the Welsh girls would get there. When I got to see all the traffic, I was petrified. I had to get across the road to Speakers' Corner. All of a sudden there was a tap on my shoulder. 'Oh,' he said, 'Fancy meeting you here.' I thought, 'There's lovely, somebody knows me.' When I turned around,

---

[11] Emrys Jones *The Welsh in London 1500–2000*. UWP 2002

there was ever such a posh gentleman standing there. I looked at him again. I thought, 'I don't know anybody well-dressed.' All I knew were the boys from the village. I looked at him, I said, 'I don't even know you!' With one gallop, I was gone!

I met my friend down there. 'Oh!' I said, 'I had such a fright.' She said, 'We mustn't talk to any of the Guards.' The Welsh Guards had a bad name. You weren't supposed to speak to them. They were after all the girls. We met the others and there was an old gentleman, he was Welsh. He was like a father to them all. We had a chat to him and he said, 'Now you look after yourselves.' We found a dance on the Edgware Road. All the Welsh people used to go there. It was called Parr's; we all used to meet there.

MARGARET D.

We used to meet some of the Welsh girls there, who had been with us in Lapswood. We'd meet in the West End. Marina and I used to have the Sunday half day together, but she stopped us then, because if she wanted to entertain, there was nobody there, so we had every other. That was understandable, as he had his surgery in Chiswick High Road and there was no one to answer phones. We didn't mind that.

We'd go to Hyde Park on Sunday. If you happened to have a Sunday half day, you'd go up to the West End and go to the chapel then, Castle Street Welsh Baptist, and they'd all congregate there. After the service then, there was the Welsh hymn singing round this big tree in Hyde Park. There'd be this minister – what's his name now, he was on the 'box' – always there on a Sunday and in the week. The Welsh people would congregate singing down there.

It would go on until eleven o'clock, but we had to be in by ten, so we always left early because we had to go by bus from the park to Victoria and catch a tube afterwards.

MARY K.

I used to go out with the little girl every afternoon. It was lovely. We used to go down by the Tower Of London. I never

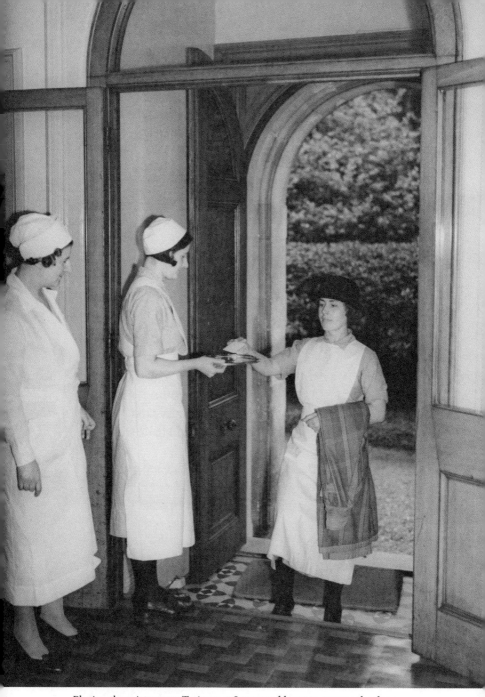

Playing the aristocracy. Trainees at Lapswood learn to answer the door.

went in there though! I took her down and sat on the bench there. There was another park where a friend from home came down to see me, all the way from Hampstead. 'Oh,' she said, 'This is a terrible place. Why don't you come up to work in Hampstead?' I said, 'I will later on.'

Most of these women had lived close-knit lives within their own family circle. Their relatives would have told them stories about living in London and they would be keen to tell stories themselves on their return. One of the attractions of going away for some of them was the chance to have new experiences, to see the wider world. Living in London they could be a part of the exciting times and get to witness events that their families could only read about in the newspapers.

CEINWEN
The Duchess of Northumberland lived next door. We were allowed to go, with her staff, to look at her three daughters dressed ready to be presented at Court, with their ostrich feathers and all the palaver. We had some good times, you know, but I was very homesick all the time, very homesick.

HAZEL
The Cohens were the only family I worked for. I was there three years. We had all the build-up to the War. They were helping Jews to get out. We had the Blackshirts in London, Oswald Mosley's Blackshirts, so you knew what was going on.

CEINWEN
When the Jubilee was on they sent a bottle of champagne down to the kitchen for us to have a drink and then at a certain time in the evening when the bonfire was lit in the Park, we were out all night. We were all together in Piccadilly. I'd never seen anything like it in all my life because they were playing football with the policemen's helmets. They were sitting and standing all on top of taxis. I'd never seen anything like it. It was fabulous, but I still couldn't wait to go home.

One day I was in Hyde Park which was right across the road. I was sitting on a seat and I was accosted by a car and I never realised, because I was raw like. That was the same time that the Queen of the Belgians got killed and I was reading the news. I was reading about Queen Astrid and a car pulled up. Frightened me to death. I'll never forget that.

I went to the American Embassy. I was knocking around with the footman from there. I had a sneaky look at the Embassy. We weren't really allowed to have any friendships with men, I seen the table laid for a banquet there, with all the silver. It was fabulous. Wonderful!

MARGARET C.

We used to go to the cake shop in Wandsworth. 56 West Hill, Wandsworth, by Putney Bridge. I was up there when the King Edward affair was on. Lots of reporters used to come in the café. They used to tell us about it. But we didn't take a lot of notice of it. It was all in the papers abroad, but not here. We didn't know. I was in London when Crystal Palace caught fire. We were on the roof then, in West Hill, looking at the fire at Crystal Palace.

MEGAN

I think valley people were very naïve years ago. If any girl was going to London, to service, they used to say, 'When it's your day off, don't you go out in the streets, 'cos they'll stick a needle in you and you'll be abroad and you won't know where your home is after. They'll make you forget everything.' The girls believed it, they were too frightened to go out anywhere; or do anything. They wouldn't even go out to the pictures. I don't know where they had all this upheaval from.

ELIZABETH

One thing that sticks in my mind about Chelsea was the Barracks, which we could see from an upstairs window. The Pensioners were very colourful. I remember watching the guards marching, in preparation for duty at the Palace or for a parade – the twirling and turning, always in step, the shouting and barking of orders. I shall never forget such things.

MARY K.

On Saturday, the two sisters used to take me up Whitechapel shopping. At night they used to slim. They said, 'We're going to have to keep fit tonight.' They had too much food to eat so we'd have all this exercise business in the lounge there!

Having older sisters also in London was of great benefit and many would take every opportunity to meet up and do things together.

HAZEL

My sister was very good to me. Although we quarrelled as children, while she was working for the Courtaulds, she was really very good, very, very good. She earned much more money than I did and we often met in Marble Arch. She would take me to the Lyons Corner House and treat me to tea; and always a hot milk drink before we went home.

It was a long way for her to come in from Eltham. We arranged to meet in Marble Arch, 'cos I could walk up Bayswater Road. She used to come on the tube. We always had to be in by ten, there were no late nights or anything.

MAY

I used to meet my sister on my days off and eventually she got married up in London.

I never heard any swear words at home, but I remember someone saying the four letter word. I thought to myself, I know I don't know much English, but somebody told me that I wouldn't find it in the dictionary. When I said to my sister when I met her, and we still spoke in Welsh, when we met. I said, 'What does this **** mean?' She said, 'Where did you hear that?' 'They're using it.' She just gave me a clip, on the underground. 'It doesn't matter what you heard. You're not supposed to say it.'

A girl in our bedroom said something about lesbians. I thought, I don't know, I'm hearing things. I told Nance, 'They are saying something terrible in the Club. They are coming out with this "lesbians". She said, 'If you don't know anything about it, then shut up!' So I still didn't know what a lesbian was. I don't think I knew until the last twenty years!

The cinema was at the height of its popularity between the Wars, and despite the Depression, attendance was high. It provided the much-needed escapism from humdrum and hard lives. Many people would go regularly every week, regardless of the film that was being shown. It was the highlight of their working week.

MARGARET C.

I didn't enjoy London itself, not really. Mary and I used to go to the pictures, in the High Street on our half day. Mrs Ellwood's two grandsons were living with her then and their parents. They used to say, 'We're going to treat Mary and you to the pictures, tonight.' I used to say, 'Ooo, that's good. Two young men (they were only twelve and fourteen) taking us to the pictures.' It was ever so cheap. We would go down Wembley High Street. It wasn't far. I used to be friendly with some of the customers that come into the café. I got friendly with their wives. I used to go to one in Harlesden. They used to invite me out, now and again for tea. I was quite content where I was, if I could read. We had good conversations.

HAZEL

We often arranged to have the same half day, if we could. We would walk London and if she could afford it, my sister would treat me to a boat ride down the River Thames. And if we could afford it, we would go up Edgware Road to the cinema.

There were two cinemas in Edgware Road where you could go quite cheaply. Two pence to go in. I'd save my money for the winter because in the summer you could go to Hyde Park, or Kensington Gardens. Or, if it was nice and warm, we would go down to the Serpentine. You had the music hall also, in Edgware Road. We saw Sophie Tucker and all the big stars. We'd go up in the gods to hear those. But if my sister had a little bit of extra money, she would treat me. There was a big cinema in Marble Arch, which we had to pay half a crown to get in. That was half my week's wages! Or there was one in Tottenham Court Road. Those big cinemas were worth that extra money because you had a good film, then you had a stage show. Edmundo Ross, Joe Loss, all the big stage bands played on that stage. Then you had the big film afterwards, so you really had your 2/6 worth.

MARY K.

My mistress's brother was in Stepney and he had a maid from Treherbert, the next village to Treorchy. They said, 'They've come to fetch you today, to take you out.' Sunday, going to the pictures! Pictures on a Sunday! 'Oh dear', I thought, 'I've never heard of that.' Anyway four of us went to Stepney and were sitting in the pictures, and there were some boys behind us. They were pushing us, pulling our hair. They heard us talking and they were taking the mickey out of us apparently. I said, 'I'm going to get the attendant.' I was afraid that they might attack us when we got outside. Anyway we came out and my friends took me right back where I was staying. Eleven o'clock I had to be in.

MARY W.

I had a night off now and went to the pictures. But I had to be in at ten. I sat down and saw the picture through. Oh no, it was ten o'clock! It was 'God Save the King'. The old King then. I got up and a lady said, 'You can't walk out when they're playing 'God Save the King'! In the confusion, I did get out and got on a bus. I didn't know where I was. I said to the driver, 'I want to get to Frognall Lane, West Hampstead.' He said to me. 'We're going back and we'll drop you off at the top of Finchley.' Dark, big trees up there. They dropped me on the top, and then I had to get back. I was late. She was waiting for me. I said, 'I'm sorry, I went to the pictures and the lady wouldn't let me get out and I got on the wrong bus.' 'Don't you tell your lies!' she said. 'I'm not in the habit of telling lies, Madam!'

If they had been regular chapel or church goers at home then many of them continued the practice. Very often their employers would encourage them to go as it was a safe outing and they were unlikely to get into any mischief. It would also reflect well on the employer to have a chapel-going maid.

HAZEL

I had a half day a week and one half day on a Sunday. Every other Sunday I had to go to church, a very high church, just around the corner in St Peter's Square. Quite often I mitched because Kensington Gardens were just opposite us, where the royalty lives today. You had Peter Pan's statue and the big Round Pond, where they all used to put the little boats out. I spent quite a lot of time there when I should have been in church. The Cohens were Jewish, but they weren't Conform Jews.

Mrs London said I had to go to church, so to church I went. I was church anyhow. My father was church, though my mother was Welsh Baptist. I just went. You would go in and no one would talk to you. I asked if there were Girl Guides and Brownies. They just sort of looked at you; they knew you were a domestic, private. I was now working for aristocracy. There was that difference. Even the young policemen looked up to you, believe it or not. It was extraordinary.

HILDA

There was no chapel there so I used to go to church. There were no lights in the village, no lights anywhere. The church was in the country, so I found in the bicycle shed a lantern with a candle in it. I used to light this candle and walk along the country lanes and when I came to the church, put the candle underneath the seat of the porch, so I could go to church. Oh dear! Looking back it wasn't much fun, was it?

DOROTHY

I went to chapel every Sunday, with my aunt. Whitefields, I think it was called. I liked it. We used to go up to the gallery. They had an organ and they always had a soloist there. They had a lovely minister. I used to look at him. Oh, he was lovely. I wished he would take me out!

PHYLLIS

I went to Catholic chapel once at Christmas time, with one of the girls, and I met a boy, one of the waiters, who was Irish. His mother would never give in to him marrying a Christian, English girl, but he was very nice. I met her. He took me to tea with her in the Strand in 'Paddy's shop'. It was an Irish café. She was very nice and I bought her a chain and she bought me something, but she wasn't willing for Paddy to marry.

The more gregarious of the women found it easy to make new friends, especially if they were living in institutions such as clubs or schools. If they worked with other staff or there could be other maids in the street that they might befriend, then they did not feel as isolated from society.

PHYLLIS

The rest of the evening, what was left, was our own. You'd have a little snack mind before you'd go to bed or if you were going across to a pub behind our place. A lot of servants used to gather at this place so that was how we made friends.

ELIZABETH

I had one afternoon a week off when I was able to contact those from home who were in the same position as myself. Some were not so fortunate as me, but the fact of just meeting made us all a little less homesick. No one ever referred to my being Welsh. I was small, dark and pretty, very nifty on my feet and got on with most people.

However if you lived out in the country then time could hang heavy on your hands when it was your day off. Transport was as scarce then in the country as it is now and these girls at fourteen were still minors in the eyes of the law. Their employers were *in loco parentis* so would naturally want to know where they were.

EILEEN

I used to have half a day a week, but I was too young to go out. So through the winter months, about three o'clock in the afternoon when you'd be finished on your half day, you just changed into your other clothes and sat in the kitchen with a book. In the summer, they did let me walk around the garden and I could sit out in a chair in the big back yard, but if one of the family passed by, I had to stand up as they passed by me. I know it sounds incredible but this is what happened. You had to work a year before you had a holiday.

HILDA

You were working and on call most of the time and you didn't have the freedom of going out. You only had a half day a week and then every other Sunday, something like that. We couldn't go anywhere really. We had to walk a mile and a half to the bus and it took me nine months to save for a bike. I had very little money of course. It was such a different life to my valley life – lonely, very lonely. It was hard. I cried, I think, for the first month. Baby! Cook was my cousin so at least I knew somebody. I wouldn't have gone otherwise, not at that stage, not at that age. I wouldn't have gone.

Chapter 10

Reasons for Leaving

MANY OF THESE women worked for a number of employers before they gave up domestic service. On average they had two jobs each. Mary had forty-three jobs in one year and in contrast Miriam worked very happily for four-and-a-half years with one employer – until the cook became a drinker and started to cause friction amongst the other staff. There were plenty of jobs to be had so the women could afford to be choosy. The amount and type of work that servants were expected to do at this time is anathema to us today. The tasks that they were set were very often work for work's sake and once staff were unavailable, because of the outbreak of the War, many of the tasks went undone – like the daily scrubbing of the front steps and the frequent washing of the paintwork. Their former mistresses were not prepared to spend hours on unrewarding and mundane tasks.

There were many different reasons why the girls left their employment. Some of them were not prepared to put up with poor conditions or unkind employers. Leaving home at fourteen meant that they were not really old enough to be independent and or mature enough to endure long periods away from home. Ceinwen was permanently homesick for the two years she spent working for the Duchess of Grafton.

CEINWEN

I did come home on holiday. After two years I went home, but I couldn't stay at home. I had to get out and find another job.

Her second posting was in Birmingham working for doctors who had a young family. She had started to grow up a bit by then and had a steady boyfriend so the environment would have seemed more familiar and cosy. She had day-to-day contact with the family, in contrast to being stuck in a basement washing dishes and cleaning game.

Some employers had no empathy with the young girls and made life intolerable for them. It speaks highly of their fortitude that they were prepared to stick it out for so long. Very often they were in debt to their employers so could not leave until that was cleared and they had saved enough to go home.

HILDA

He was German and she was, unfortunately, how can I say . . . very fond of her glass of wine, which ended in her becoming more or less an alcoholic. In the two years I was there it became worse and worse. Our treatment got worse and worse; it was dreadful in the end. She took the key of the larder and instead of having a full ration, we had to share this ration. I became quite ill after two years. I came down to about six stone three; eventually I had to come home.

I was virtually being starved and Mrs Tillet didn't really know. She wasn't responsible, put it that way. I think she was around fifty years old. He was very nice, but I don't think he was aware of it, so we both left. I supposed it caused some trouble for her and suffered eventually, we found later on,

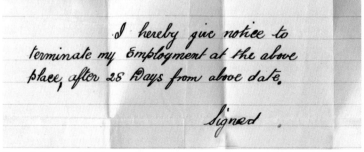

I hereby give notice to terminate my Employment at the above place, after 28 Days from above date.

signed .

Enough is enough! A letter of resignation.   (Glamorgan Archives)

years later . . . something called DTs? We didn't understand what was going on. We were chapel girls, Methodist, teetotal. My mother made her own wine, but that was one thing. Most people did for medicinal purposes, they say! We weren't used to it at all.

I was away a year before I came home. Things weren't too bad and I hoped they would get better, naturally. But after the second year it was something we just couldn't take. She started accusing you of doing this or doing that; or taking this or taking that. Looking back now, she couldn't help it, could she? So we both left and I was home nine months then, trying to get well again.

EILEEN

Anyway time come for me to go home. As soon as my father saw me he said, 'You're not going back there!' I had to go to the doctor because I was very anaemic. My clothes came home in a sack, what I had left behind.

I was home for a little while then. My granny came down on holiday from the Isle of Wight. She gave my mother a row as she thought she had done wrong. 'You weren't sent to London until you were sixteen and you sent her at fourteen.'

MARY K.

She was interviewing now. She was going to have a couple, husband and wife, so I said to Gladys, 'We'll have to get a job now.'

She must have given us a reference, because we got a job at a cookery college for ladies, but we were in a house over the road and we had to go and clean. It was housework, but we had to sleep over there, in the freezing cold.

Anyway, she interviewed this couple, husband and wife. We left. She wouldn't have Welsh girls anymore. We had a message then from the couple: 'Are you the two that who were at that house?' I said, 'Yes. I let you in to be interviewed.' 'Oh', they said, 'We can't stay there.'

I discovered afterwards that she was mental or had something wrong with her the way she used to carry on. We used to do our work and we used to get on alright. I went home then for Christmas and I didn't go back into service. I had sisters then. My sisters were fifteen and sixteen. Then I worked in factories.

Of all the women Phyllis was the only one that mentioned what we would call today sexual harassment. Whether the others had been lucky or were not prepared to talk about it, I heard nothing about any sexual misdemeanours. Because these women volunteered to speak to me I think that those who suffered in this way just did not volunteer to meet me. It is not likely that if you had been persuaded to have sexual adventures, whilst in service, that you would want to tell a complete stranger about them, fifty years on.

During my visits to clubs and organisations where I have given a talk based on these findings, a number of ladies have approached me and told me of their mother's or grandmother's experiences. Some of these stories are worth repeating, even if they are second-hand.

Marj told me that her Aunty Jane went into service and eventually became a cook. She became pregnant by a man in the house. She made a bargain with the family and swore never to tell who it was – the master or the son – and in return they would educate the child. She had the baby and remarkably stayed on in her situation. When the little boy was thirteen, he was sent to a military academy and eventually became a major in the army. Aunty Jane later married and went on to have more children. Her husband always said that he had married a 'widow' woman.

Another lady told me that her Aunty Sarah went into service at a farm and became pregnant by the son of the house. He got another girl pregnant at the same time so Aunty Sarah's mother would not let her marry him although the wayward son asked her to. A little girl was born and was adopted by another sister who could not have children. The father married the other pregnant girl but never paid any maintenance to Aunty Sarah for her little girl.

Twice I've been told by the person who approached me after my talk that their mothers did not know who their fathers were. One of the grandmothers came home pregnant and the matter was never discussed. The other lady told me how the fact of being illegitimate blighted her mother's life as a child, because the grandmother subsequently got married and the girl was shunted around the homes of various aunts. Money arrived for the girl from a mysterious source and so she was better dressed than her contemporaries and consequently bullied by them for being different.

Phyllis began to feel uneasy in her situation:

> I can't say how long I stuck this now. I stuck it for a while. They were telling me that I was a pretty girl at that age. Anyway the boss would always linger behind, when everybody used to get up from their lunch. They would go and he would linger and try and put me on his lap. I knew that was wrong; I was getting scared. I said I would have to leave; I didn't give the reason why, but I left there.

Sometimes it was the other members of staff that made their lives difficult.

DOROTHY

> In the afternoon, he came up and brought two oranges and two apples and two pears. I said, 'What are these for?' 'They're for you.' I didn't have to put them on my housekeeping list. They were payment for my Irish stew. I just left them on the sideboard. This nanny, an Irish nanny, she was a bitch, she was. She came down and said, 'Oh, you've got fruit here have you?' With that she caught hold of the bag and took out a pear, and apple and an orange. I said, 'Pardon me! They're mine.' 'Oh no they're not.' 'They are not on the bill,' I said. 'They are my property!' But she didn't take any notice and went upstairs.
>
> So when Mrs Tan (that was her name) came home, I told her about it. I said, 'Her cheek. They were my property. If you

would like to look at the list, the housekeeping list, you can see.' I didn't like that about Mrs Tan. She didn't say, 'Oh I quite believe you.' She took the list into the dining room and she perused it and examined it. When she came out she said, 'You're quite right. It's not on the list.' 'I told you it wasn't on the list. I am not a liar. By the way, you can take my notice at the same time! "What!' 'Yes,' I said, 'You can take it.' She came round coaxing me to stay on, offered me more money and everything. I said, 'I won't work with that nanny. 'Queenie can't get nannies, that's the trouble. I can't sack her very well.' 'No, I'll go,' I said.

MIRIAM

I came home. The cook was a bit of a drinker and she started causing a lot of trouble. She used to set us one against the other. In the end I got sick of it. I said, 'Right. I've had enough of this.' I'm not quarrelsome. I went to Mrs Benson, that was the lady I worked for, and I had to give month's notice. Oh, she was awful upset, 'Perhaps you'll come back?' 'No', I said, 'I won't come back.' And I left then, only because she used to put us against one another. We weren't like that.

Elizabeth had an unusual reason for leaving and it also illustrates that there were very caring employers as well as heartless ones:

After six months at Kensington Gore, the boss died. The housekeeper was instructed to take particular care of anybody employed in his household under the age of eighteen years, and to be sure that such persons were found employment only in a Christian home. The housekeeper was satisfied that this was so.

That is how I came to be working for a Mrs Stanley in a charming little house in Chelsea. A cook and parlour maid were already there and I took great care not to finish up at the kitchen sink, so I was a housemaid and that suited me fine.

Hazel's situation changed within the house as the result of the resignation of former colleagues who were not replaced:

22 Esmond Gardens.
Bedford Park W.4.
18th June 1928.

Dear Mrs Dunn,

You will I am sure be glad to hear I am very pleased with Edith. When she arrived I expected a girl of 18 so I was a little shocked to find out she was under 18, however I took to her at once, and although new brooms usually sweep clean. I think that if Edith continues as she has started she will turn out an excellent maid. She is very clean which appeals to me, painstaking a good worker & very cheerful. I am giving her very good wages for a girl of her age, so I hope she will not let me train her & then leave me.

When Edith arrived her feet were hurting her, on examination I found the new shoes had caused a couple of nasty places on the bridge of her big toes. I dressed them, but they did not heal, so I took her to the Doctors & he attended to her toes I expect they will be quite healed in a day or two. The Dr. thoroughly examined Edith as she had a bad cold & as a result was a little deaf The Dr. says her tonsils must be attended to, otherwise she will always have nasty colds so I am going to ask you to get them done when she comes home for her holidays. If they are done directly she gets home they will be quite right in a few days.

Edith appears as happy as the day long & already thinks she is better off than Sophie, anyway I think I have obtained a nice little girl who will appreciate a good home, only I must not spoil her.

Yours truly.
M. W. Gedge.

A caring employer gives a maid's family reassurance, whilst also expecting loyalty.
(by kind permission of Dilwyn Morgan)

After three years I left because when the under maid left, the house maid left. She left to get married and the under house maid left because war was becoming imminent. They left to go home. Lady Cohen didn't employ any other extra people. The lady's maid was still there; she was now having to do the house maid's work as well. I can always remember that I had to go upstairs before everybody else and I did what was the gentleman's toilet. Clean that and the cloakroom. I thought this is not on. I wasn't getting any extra money. There were little duties that were becoming extra to me.

Mary K. was unlucky to find herself in a family where she had no support.

What happened, when I went to a lovely big house not far from Hampstead Heath, oh, I ran away from there! There was no mother there again. There was just the two daughters and the father. It was hard work. Oh I had to scrub the steps. The tradesmen used to say. 'You won't be here long, kid. They change their staff every month.'

Only two of the women mentioned that they were actually dismissed and coincidentally both were told to leave because of the fear of illness. May had gone to the South Coast as a children's nurse when she was fourteen.

I stayed there about six weeks. That was enough. I had a cough and they said it was through malnutrition that we suffered while we were at home. It could be. I don't think so. I will say of my mother that we never felt hungry. Everything was homemade, but no cooking on a Sunday though.

One suspects that the family for whom she was working made the excuse of malnutrition when they probably suspected that she had TB, which was rife in the valleys of South Wales at this time.

MARY K.

My aunt died of TB and when my cousin took me up Treorchy cemetery, I had a shock. Somebody in later years, must have been one of my uncles (he was a bachelor) had a stone put up, with his mother and father and I had four aunties that I didn't know about. They must have died before they were thirty. I had such a shock, because they never talked about that part. They all had TB.

At fourteen May was just the right age to have it.

Phyllis's dismissal was more puzzling because her employer at that time was an old lady with arthritis.

With her permission I used to go up and see my sister, if she was going out. I went up one day and the children had scarlet fever. My sister's people had gone out as well, but we didn't think there would be anything wrong.

I said to my employer that I had met up at my sister's. Innocently enough I said, 'The children have got scarlet fever.' That was it, I had to go! She was afraid that she would catch it at her age, in her state, so I had to go.

It was very common for the family back home to require the girls to return when there was a crisis, sometimes a death, often illness and some cases a new baby.

MARGARET C.

I left Mrs Ellwood when she went to stay with her daughter in Batavia and then she went to her other daughter's, who also lived in London. I wasn't too keen on that part of London. I said I would go home and think about going back. My father died in 1937 and I didn't go back.

EUNICE

When I was in Wiltshire, I had to give a month's notice. My father couldn't write, or he wouldn't write, let's put it that way, so my mother had to write. She told me to give a month's notice. 'Dad said I was to come home.' He did come up and fetch me at the end of the notice. Why, I don't know, because I had gone up on my own. Then when I was in Cathedral Road I only had to give a week's notice. They didn't want me to leave. Dr Arwen Evans said, 'Look, I can get you off this war work because you are working for a doctor.' But no, I wanted to stop housework.

MAY

My mother had a nervous breakdown. There was no asking to come home. My father didn't feel that he had a right to, but I came home. I knew that out of £5 I had saved, I had to do something, so I opened a shop in the front room. My mother taught me how to do the toffee and I used to do all types of toffee – mint toffees, toffee dabs, toffee apples, coconut, peanuts.

NANCY

At the end of the year my father was getting quite frightened about me being away. My mother really wanted to make sure that it was nursing that I wanted to do, so she said, 'Put your notice in and come home. We'll get you a job with children. You like children. We'll see if you enjoy looking after children.' So she did. She got me a job locally, looking after twins. I had only been there a couple of months when they were packed off to school. At this time my mother wasn't awfully well and my father said, 'I think you'd better come home and look after things at home.' I did.

Phyllis was persuaded by her sister to move closer to her and unfortunately it did not work out as planned and she ended up working for a dirty, idle woman.

After I was there, I can't say exactly how long, my sister then said to me that her Mrs's daughter was looking for a maid.

'Why don't you come and work for her? We could be all together.' 'I don't like leaving these people. They're nice to me. I'm quite happy here,' I said. 'If you come, her daughter comes down to stay with her mother for hours, and she'll be bringing the baby down. We'll have a lot of time together,' she said. I didn't want to. I really didn't want to, but she finally persuaded me and I thought I wouldn't be so lonely. It was only half day a week you got, that was your only time off.

On occasion the women changed their jobs just because they wanted a change of scene; they needed a new stimulus and in all probability thought that the grass was greener elsewhere.

DOROTHY

I was here for a couple of years and I had no complaints about it. It was a smashing job, but my friend went to Cardiff; she was a parlour maid and she wrote up to say they wanted a cook there. 'How about coming down there, Dorothy? It will be nice company and it will be a change for you.' So I left because I thought Cardiff would be a bit of a change.

PHYLLIS

My sister had to come home and eventually I was in London on my own. I thought I don't know anybody, so I came home for a break. But I came back to London.

MARY K.

I gave my notice. I thought I'd go up to West Hampstead to work for the Jews up there. I found a post as a cook, cook general. I had only done plain cooking. I gave my notice and they said, 'We're sorry to lose you, but come down to see us, any time.' Master Jack, he was looking for a wife, he was. The Jewish people used to go around the houses to match them. I don't know what they called him. I heard them saying, 'Tell me, are there any Jewish girls in Wales?' 'Nobody would have him!' I said. I was getting cheeky by now.

Doris was simply lonely working in a house after being in a school.

> There was three of us working there. The cook, the house
> maid and I was the parlour maid. I had to look after the old
> gentleman. I used to see to his room; light his fire for him
> and clean the rest of the house of course. And serve in the
> dining room because I was the parlour maid. There weren't
> the people there to have the fun. It's a quiet place Chepstow, I
> stayed there for just twelve months.

Mary W. left for the most poignant and tragic of reasons:

> I left because of an incident. I did get friendly with a boy in the
> next village and he got killed on his motorbike. One night one
> of the girls came in and they said, 'There's been an accident
> outside one of the drives.' Me and this other girl went to have
> a look. There was this body there, lying on the side of the road.
> This boy I was friendly with, he had those certain boots; he
> was very proud of them. The body was covered and I could see
> these boots sticking out and I realised it was him. It seemed,
> when he was on the motorbike, the handles came in contact
> with the hedge and he went over the handle bars and broke
> his neck.
>
> He had been working in Blandford in a shop. I can't actually
> remember how I met him. It might have been when he came
> to bring groceries. It was such a long time ago. I would have
> been about eighteen probably. So I didn't want to stay after
> that.

Phyllis was indignant when she was accused of stealing and chose
to leave in protest.

> She [the landlady] had a big bar in the pub, and they showed
> me what to do, with the drawing and serving. They never
> used a till. They had very big smoking rooms. When an
> order came I would take it in on a tray. I did that for some
> time: bring the money back and put it in the till. It wasn't all

scientific like we've got now. It was straightforward: press the button and put the money in.

I hadn't been there long and I was accused of cheating. I couldn't understand how I could be cheating; it just didn't strike a cord with me. How could I be cheating? Because you'd go out, they would give you your order, you'd come straight in. I wasn't as clever as the others. What they were doing was taking the order, a large order, for they were huge smoking rooms – taking these drinks out but only coming in and ringing so much on the till and pocketing the money. I didn't understand about anything like that. I was accused of doing that. That was it. I packed up and I left and I came home.

Doris felt out of it with her friends and she too had a tragic tale to tell.

I suppose I had made friends there and I was going out with these friends, but when I brought another friend in, there were three of us. I couldn't go out with one and then go out with the other. I was sort of in between. I thought the best thing was to go. There was a fellow there, he worked in the kitchen and he was very fond of me. I knew that I wouldn't go out with him or anything. When I used to be coming down the aisle with the basket and he'd been out for his half day, the day before, he would throw a bar of chocolate in my basket. All the girls that night would be after me to share my chocolate. The day I left, he saw me to the bus and he cried his eyes out. He wrote to me and he got his mother writing to me, but then of course the war came and he joined the Navy and his ship went down. End of story.

The outbreak of World War Two is a distinctive watershed in terms of much of our social history. Nearly half of the women left for that reason; In some cases the war coincided with their marriage. Unbeknown at the time, the War also ended domestic service as it had been recognised for the past three hundred odd years.

War meant that they left London for the safety of Wales, to do work of national importance.

MARGARET C.
Then I come back to Cardiff. There was a talk of war and one thing and another. They said I either had to go into the forces or get a factory job. You could get factory jobs then and I went over Spillers, the flour factory. I wasn't there twelve months, by then my chest was playing up. Currans was opening for munitions so I was there five years. I was there when it opened and there when it closed.

MARGARET D.
They all cleared out from London then, a lot of girls went back home, when there were signs of war. It was a good thing too, seeing the way they bombed London. The war came then, and that's how I came back. My family would have been on pins if I was up there. I've never, ever been back to London since.

EUNICE
When the war came, I was working in Cathedral Road, Cardiff. As soon as I was sixteen I had to register for war work. My grandfather who was living with us said, 'You don't want to be going to a munitions factory. Go down the Sheds. (That was the name of the Caerphilly Railway Workshops.) Go and see Bill Matthews and tell him I sent you.' I made an appointment and went down. He said, 'Who sent you?' 'My grandfather, James Elsbury.' 'Start Monday!' So I started there helping to repair railway engines.

DORIS
Then the War came and the bombing started so I thought it was time to come home. I told this Mrs Williams that I wanted to leave. She said, 'I'm not accepting it. No! I had to write it out. I wrote my notice out and handed it to her and she had to take it then. I came back home.

MIRIAM

When I came back to Ponty, I went to Cardiff to work, near Llandaff Cathedral. I worked for Mrs G there. She was an old lady. I didn't like it much. She had one son that wasn't very well. They had a nurse for him. Everything in the house was all parquet flooring and it was jolly hard work. I was on my own most of the time there.

When the War started, I used to come home every week because it was only 1/6 return then. The nurse was very good; she used to say, 'Here's your fare home.' I used to come home and when the air raids started all the buses would stop. I started to get bronchitis. I got so bad in the end that I had to pack my job in.

ANNIE

When the War broke out, I went home as I was frightened. Then I went to a job in a factory but it was dreadful. I stayed there for a day, a morning. It was a really dirty place. After that I had a job with Mrs C, in Canton, Cardiff. They had an ice-cream parlour. I finally left service because I had had enough of domestic service. I joined the Land Army. It was very hard, but it was quite a lot of fun as well.

HAZEL

I was down in Littleton-on-Sea, when war was declared. I came back. I tried to join the forces straight away, but they took one look at me at the Air Ministry in London and said, 'How old are you?' I said, 'I'll soon be eighteen.' 'Very sorry, you come back to us when you are eighteen.'

I gave my notice into Lady Cohen. She said, 'You can't possibly go. I'll inform the Air Ministry.' 'I'm sorry but my mother has given me permission. May I stay until the end of April?' 'No!' So I had to leave at the end of March. Fortunately for me, my godmother now had come up to London to live with her sister, in the flat opposite Holloway Prison. There was me not seventeen, not quite seventeen, sleeping between two old ladies! But you just didn't think about it. I was very glad to have somewhere to go, very glad. I joined the forces, joined the WAFs, on 1 May 1940

Hilda's experience of when the War came gives a superb picture of the general upheaval created in people's lives; how the whole country was put on a war footing and how disruptive that was. There was no choice, no argument, no alternative and particularly no complaining, you just had to get on with life as best you could.

When the War came we had to do work of national importance. It was very difficult because we couldn't leave our domestic job without somewhere to live. The military gave us no alternative but to put twenty soldiers on the top floor of the house – the Twelfth Royal Lancers – with the result we servants had to move down a floor and I was then sleeping in the most luxurious room, with a four poster bed with curtains, called the Japanese Room! It was wonderful.

That went on for quite a while. Then the Lancers moved out and the Derbyshire Yeomanry moved in. They wanted more room still, so they moved us out entirely. They moved Miss Heron in to a little gardener's cottage. The head parlour maid, she moved out with me. It was dreadful. There was no bathroom, no electric light. We had to have lamps; no hot water. After living in a large house with all the facilities, you could imagine what it was like.

We were given the alternative then of working in a brick yard or working as domestics in Dorking Hospital, or in the munitions factory. The munitions factory was the nearest and that was three miles away. I chose that. We were working until quite late and had to come home then, light a fire and cook our meals. It seemed dreadful after having a cook to do your meals for you and sitting down to a lovely table with seven companions.

Getting married was a popular reason for leaving amongst domestic servants. It was not unheard of for a girl to opt for marriage rather than stay in service, a form of escape from the tyranny of drudgery. Unless you remained living locally there was no choice but to leave as the post would have usually been a live-in one. Wives were expected to stay at home once they were married, even in quite poor households.

MARY W.

After I came back to the Rhondda I eventually went to a place on Newport Road, Cardiff, to a Dr Wallace. I stayed there under a year and I left there and I went with Mr and Mrs Cotham, in Palace Road, Llandaff. I stayed there for six years. I left when I got married.

EILEEN

I stayed with them until I was twenty and I married Maurice, the butcher's boy on 19 July 1939. My mother came down and my father, and that was the first holiday my father had with pay, because if they didn't work Easter holiday, a bank holiday, it was deducted from their wages. It was either 1938 or 1939 that miners had their first holiday with pay. My mother made me a white wedding dress and a dress for my sister and Maurice's youngest sister. I had two bridesmaids. I was married in Pyle Street Methodist Church, in Newport, Isle of Wight. Dr and Mrs Balfour came to my wedding.

Chapter 11

The End of an Era

G OING INTO SERVICE? We have shared the experiences of twenty women living in Wales so now can understand a little of what it meant. They left home with the hope of a better existence than their mother's. As a servant, they might have eaten better, dressed better, slept more comfortably than at home. In some cases they tried to put a bit by or send a few shillings home. A girl who had been in service was more marriageable since she had more housewifely skills.

> NELLIE
> My mother insisted that I went into service. Her saying was that you go into service and make yourself a good wife for a man another day.

It was a job for women between home and marriage as it indeed prepared them for domesticity. All the respondents married, except Miriam. Ceinwen, Nellie, Eileen, Dorothy, May, Morddfa, Phyllis, Mary W. and Elizabeth were all married from service. Morddfa even recalled her former employer sending her a wedding present.

A servant was able to earn her keep and those few pennies might make all the difference to her family's survival. It offered both a wage and a roof over their heads unlike factory work. Sending a girl into service was frequently chosen by parents as the best thing for their children. For many girls, going into service was their only chance of seeing the world and escaping the poverty at home.

DOROTHY

One morning I woke up – I looked at the wallpaper and I thought it was dots on the wallpaper. I kept looking at them. 'I'm sure those dots are moving.' I stood up on the bed and I see that they were little flat things moving. There was a smell. My mother lived two doors away. I went to her. She was a very clean woman; we never had anything like that. I told her about them and described them and she said, 'Well, that sounds to me as if she has got bugs.' 'Well, Mum, there were dozens, they were crawling all over the wall.' Yet if you went into the house, you would think it was very clean. I found them in the baby's cupboard and in her clothes and everything, I cleaned the kids for her, because I kept at them until I had nothing out.

I was only thirteen then. I got paid 15s for five weeks' work. I got food as well but I had to do all the cooking for them, ready for by the time he got home. He worked in the mines, you see. My mother did the washing.

In the literature on the employment of women during the inter-war period, it is never really stressed how important domestic service was in creating an opportunity for women to have a life outside their families and communities.

HAZEL

They had a house in Littlestone-on-Sea, in Kent, which is just outside Folkestone, on the New Romney line. We went down there in the summer. We used to go down by train. It was a kerfuffle, all the luggage had to go there. We enjoyed that. It was still the same conditions: seen-and-not-heard sort of thing. We had a chef down there so Mrs London didn't come.

HILDA

Now at the end of the billiard room, there was a little place, built on, incorporated in the house, and called the Flower Room. The gardener used to bring me flowers, twice a week, to arrange in the different rooms. I didn't have any training, but I love flowers and I love growing them. I had to help my father in the allotments during the time I left school. I've always loved flowers. When I was little, buttercups in an egg cup would give me joy! It was a wonderful life. I wasn't allowed to go to the garden to pick flowers but I had the most wonderful vases and containers to use, as you can imagine.

I loved doing the flowers, arranging the table to match whatever was going on – like there was a huge container with legs, something like you would put a wedding cake on, but it had a mirror. You could put beautiful flowers on there and it would reflect.

MIRIAM

Mind, the four-and-a-half years I spent in service I don't regret, because it showed me which knives and forks to use when you go out, as well as how to do the cooking, how to do the cleaning, various things. I quite enjoyed it.

It was just before the War started, so that we came in contact with a lot of Germans. They sent to Austria and that because they couldn't get domestics here then. I think Hitler had gone into Austria and took them over, so I was with a few of them. Very, very interesting. They came over here to speak English and what not and get out of Hitler's way, I suppose. They were quite nice, some of them.

Where I lived there were all private farms, all owned by people with money. They used to have beautiful Jersey cows. We had wonderful food. All the meats and everything were supplied by the butchers. They'd kill their own. The place was so lovely. The food now is nothing like the food we had then. The milk was that thick with cream. When we wanted cream we used to put it in a big dish and just skim it off and you would have yellow, yellow cream. If we ran out of milk, we used to go over the road to get it.

The scullery maid used to live locally. The others were

Welsh. I enjoyed it. It was hard work, but I enjoyed it. I bought a bike because transport was scarce. We only had a bus about once an hour, so I cycled everywhere on my own. I used to go to Staines, Egham, Windsor, Virginia Water, all round there. Very beautiful place. I used to go through the Windsor Park and Windsor and Eton was just down the street from there. If you went to Sunninghill, you could go into Camberley, where the soldiers were. When you went through Ascot, then you went to Bracknell. I used to cycle everywhere; I enjoyed it.

ELIZABETH

I saw another side of life; a wider vision of life, if you like. I remember being home for a weekend, I was about seventeen, and coming in from a night out to find my father having his toddy. We sat together and talked. It was lovely. He asked me if I was truly happy and I assured him I was.

It may have been lowly paid and undervalued, but working away from home contributed to the girls' independence. In later life, they were all able to support and understand the expectations of their own children. Although they lost their adolescent years in a way that would not be tolerated today, they gained a wider vision of the world and we, as women, are as much their inheritors as we are of the Suffrage Movement.

EUNICE

London wasn't so bad in those days as it is today. Even so, it was bad enough. The children today, of fourteen, they wouldn't do it.

As stated earlier, the employers had absolute control over their servants. This control helped to define the class structure and ensured that the servants knew their place. Frequently, however there was a very thin line, in social terms, between the employer and the employee, especially in single servant homes.

One lady who contacted me from Aberdeen, and was not included in the study, told me how her employers paid a man to teach the young servants during the evenings. At first I was very impressed by this altruistic gesture, but on thinking more deeply about it, it occurred to me that this could have been a form of control. By occupying their spare time, however wisely, the employers were ensuring that the servants did not have opportunities to get into mischief and become troublesome. I am inclined to give these particular employers, however, the benefit of the doubt as they eventually sent her to teachers' training college and educated her son at private school. When she was left as a young war widow, they even supported him through medical school.

When women aged 21 and over, finally gained the franchise on equal terms with men, in 1928, those older maids were able to vote alongside their mistresses. The majority of live-servants however were only minors and took no part in politics. Although in 1931 the National Conference of Labour Women, under the chairmanship of Dorothy Elliot, proposed a charter for domestic workers, reiterating the need for training, the regulation of hours of work, rate of pay, food and accommodation standards and holiday entitlement, it made no difference. A domestic servant was to be called a domestic worker; uniform was not considered necessary and should only be provided by the employer, and the cap, which was a 'badge of servility' served no purpose.

This was the same year as Margaret Bondfield who had been Minister of Labour, the first-ever woman Cabinet Minister of any party, lost her seat in Northampton at the General Election. The reason I mention this is that as a woman in that position she did nothing for her working-class sisters. Labour Party commentators saw the issue as belonging outside the sphere of industrial relations; service could never be fully politicized since conditions could not be standardized. Many books have been written about the class struggle but these hidden heroines were not represented by any political party or trade union.

The prevailing attitude was expressed by Constance Eaton, in the *Good Housekeeping* magazine in 1930:

We must not lose sight of the fact that the human being whose nature it is to obey receives just as much pleasure from obeying and serving as the person born to command receives from giving orders. There is no getting away from the fact that those who serve will always be with us.

Mrs Eaton might not have been aware of the silent rebellion going on *below stairs* as illustrated by a titbit I gleaned from a man in Treorchy Library whilst I was making some enquiries concerning this book. It adds a certain colour to the alternative attitude of the time. He remembered an old lady telling him that when she was working in a gentlemen's club in London, 'She spat in the porridge of the Prime Minister.' Certainly those in the kitchens had every opportunity to rebel in their own quiet way.

Hazel spoke of being rebellious – 'I was a bit of a rebel refusing to do a few things.'

Mary K., on giving notice, went to the police station when she was refused her wages. She even told her Jewish employer 'to go back to Jerusalem' in an argument!

Welsh girls did not have the monopoly of domestic service. Some of the women who contacted me, from other parts of Britain, reinforced the class distinction. In many parts of the country, working-class girls had few opportunities other than that of domestic service. In many cases the women I interviewed were the only Welsh member of staff and some worked in houses with six or seven servants. Ceinwen was one of seven working for the Duchess of Grafton, but was the only one from Wales. This pattern was repeated with servants coming from other parts of Great Britain. Eileen worked with a Scottish girl. English women rang me from Herne Bay and Gosport in response to my letter in the *Mature Tymes*, with stories of service. One rang from Stroud to say that she had a similar experience to Welsh girls. Between the ages of fourteen and eighteen she worked locally and one employer actually boxed her ears. Eventually she moved to Surrey and became a lady's maid for a titled person where 'Life was so different, everything was great.'

Fourteen of the respondents said that they enjoyed the whole experience. Elizabeth's observations, and hers was a written testimony without the benefit of my probing, were typical of those who appreciated life in service:

> There was such lovely furniture and house things, it was a joy to look after it all.

Like many of us, some of the Welsh women I spoke to genuinely loved cleaning and polishing. Nothing like a job well done to give satisfaction! Hilda and Elizabeth deeply appreciated the opportunity of living in large comfortable households. Only Mary K. moved from domestic service into factory work when she was in London, until the War forcibly drove these women out into other occupations.

I found that it was purely by chance whether or not one enjoyed life in service. Those, like Eunice, who worked as single servants were generally lonely and unhappy. Those who worked in large households had many happy times and benefited in numerous ways as recalled by Hilda, Miriam and Hazel. Margaret C. even gained some of the education that she longed for. When Doris left the companionship of the boarding school and went as a maid of all work in a private house, she noticed the difference:

> I lived in Gwentland, Chepstow. I don't think the house is there now. It was a big house in nice grounds. I wasn't quite as happy there.

Some women were ashamed that they had been in service and did not like it mentioned outside the family. A lady told me that she once mentioned to a college friend that her mother had been in service and she was told off later. 'Never tell anyone that I've been in service.'

When I visited the interviewees after I had given them the transcripts of their own tape, I was surprised to learn that when their children read them it was often the first time that they had heard their mother's story. I questioned the ladies and asked them why had it remained hidden all these years, only to be told that what they had done was of 'no importance.'

In the 1930s, service was still the biggest employer of Britain's women. The demand rose with a greater number of households employing a single servant. When the opportunity did present itself girls went into the light industries, became shop assistants or elementary school teachers, but these chances were not available to the majority of working-class girls in Wales.

The women I interviewed were part of the last generation that went into service as a matter of course. Some attempt was made by successive governments to alleviate unemployment in South Wales by establishing a number of trading estates to provide more factory work. The government offered incentives to industrialists to start new factories in these distressed areas. One such company was Kayser Bondor which set up a hosiery factory, in 1938, on the decaying iron works at Dowlais Top, Merthyr Tydfil[12]. The Bonder factory proved to be such a success that more factories were built which provided many skilled and unskilled jobs suitable for women and young girls. Local factory work meant that girls no longer had to leave home and could find work in a cheerful environment surrounded by their contemporaries.

The War itself was also a great equalizer providing opportunities for both working-class men and women to reach their potential. Hazel had her moment of glory when she bumped into her former mistress, Lady Cohen whilst they were both having lunch in the Ritz.

> She couldn't say a word! I said, 'Good afternoon, your ladyship.' 'Good afternoon, sergeant.' She replied.

A gentleman I met in East Sussex told me of an amusing incident with his mother that happened during the War. Before the War they had a very pleasant girl called Beattie working in the house when they lived in Brighton. In 1940 Beattie was called up and went into the Wrens. The gentleman's mother was in the WRVS serving tea from the van to the Army and Navy in Brighton. One

---

[12] Moira Keast *The Story of Kayser Bondor*, Baldock Musuem & Local History Society, 2007

day a Wren officer, in tricorn hat, came up to the van and said to his mother, 'How nice to see you again Mrs Smith.' It was Beattie who had been commissioned!

Between 1939 and 1945 most major country houses, which relied totally on domestic servants for their smooth running, were turned over to wartime uses, whether for military occupation, to provide homes for evacuated children or to house government departments relocated from the hazards of the Blitz. Much as they had in the First World War, the male staff went into the Forces and the women either joined the auxiliaries or helped the war effort by working in munitions factories.

Post war, the old country house world could hardly expect to return to pre-war practices. A sad number of important historic buildings were abandoned, sold off and ultimately demolished. A situation described by Sir Ernest Gower in his 1950 Government Report *Houses of Outstanding Historic Interest*:

> Now owing to economic and social changes, we are faced with a disaster comparable only to that which the country suffered with the Dissolution of the Monasteries in the sixteenth century . . . There is now not the labour available for domestic service, there is not the desire to do it; and there is not the money to pay for it.'[13]

Many people were antagonistic towards domestic service after the Second World War, as after the Great War. But the social changes of the Second World War were of much greater magnitude. In 1945, popular feeling against privilege and class was expressed in the landslide victory of the Labour Government, in spite of Winston Churchill leading Britain to victory. There would be no place for skivvies in the New Jerusalem.

Margaret C. wryly observed:

---

[13] Jeremy Musson *Up and Down Stairs. The History of the Country House Servant*, John Murray 2009

I was working in Weston for a little while and they used to have in the papers – 'Welsh need not apply'. That was before the war. They were jolly glad of them after.

As a result of the 1944 Education Act there was more equality in education for girls and a greater number were able to go to grammar school than before the War. Eileen, although she passed the entrance examination the same time as her brother, was not allowed to go. It was not unheard of for a fourteen-year-old daughter to be sent into service so that her younger brother could attend a grammar school. In a number of the families, the education of male siblings was paramount. Eileen found it a particularly bitter pill to swallow. Her elder brother was already in grammar school and because of the closeness of their age, both Eileen and her younger brother sat the Eleven Plus at the same time and only the younger brother was allowed to go.

MIRIAM
My brother did exceptionally well and my sister would have done well, but my mother had no money to send her. She went in for nursing.

The debate whether intelligence is the result of nature or nurture had no place here, but I was impressed by the fact that at least eight of the interviewees' own children obtained university degrees or professional qualifications. Some were medical doctors and Phyllis, who slept on a camp bed in the kitchen, had two sons who were professors in Australia. In all the homes there were photographs in evidence of the grandchildren or nieces and nephews dressed in academic gowns.

I was interested in their attitudes to education because I was convinced that domestic service was taken up, not because they were intellectually lacking in any way or that it was the only occupation that they were capable of doing, but that it was the only one open to them. Margaret C. craved education and she was very fortunate in working and living with the family that she did.

I used to go to night school in Wood Street and I used to go to night school in South Church Street. I wanted to get as much education as I could. I studied English, writing and composition and all like that. When I was in school, we used to have spelling bees; I used to always have prizes.

Later she told me:

They moved from Penally then to London. I went with them. They taught me quite a lot. They taught me music, because one played the piano and one played the violin and we used to have lovely musical evenings. I used to sing. I used to learn all about the pizzicato and things. I used to get to know the name of the composers, which I never knew before; I really had a lot to thank them for. She taught me all about music and books to read. She picked out all the best in life. She had had all the education; educated in France, Germany and England.

They almost treated me like an adopted daughter. Yes, they were very kind too me. Miss Whitely, the one who was in the Russian Embassy working, she told me such a lot about it, because it took her three months to come home from Russia when the war broke out, the First War. She used to say when they had the big balls in the palaces, they used to get permission to get on the landing and look through the balustrade. And she said these Cossacks used to be cruel. She said it was nothing for them to ride through streets and slash with their swords and their whips. She was there when there was the Revolution in 1917. She'd seen Rasputin, Miss Whitely. She said he was horrible. The Tsarina – of course I read all about this after – the Tsarina was attracted to him.

I am strongly of the opinion that these women were cheated out of a more rewarding life by the fact that they had working-class origins. Of those who had continued to work throughout their life, several held responsible jobs. Eunice ran a children's home, May had been a quality control inspector, Doris received a pension from her time as a senior messenger with the Civil Service, Eileen became head clerk in the local office of a large insurance company and Nancy qualified as a nurse and later got a degree.

Doris too was interested in school and if she had lived in a different time and had the opportunity for more education she would have benefited in many ways. This would have also been true of thousands of working-class girls and boys throughout Britain.

DORIS

I liked going to school myself. First I was in the junior school which wasn't far for me to go. It was at the top of my street. Then we were told we had to go to the higher school, which was Treherbert. I had just over a mile to walk, down there. I did quite well at school.

In the long term, however, the economic levelling of the population was probably of great significance in removing class distinction and the idea of knowing one's place. Death duties and taxes eroded the private fortunes of the landed gentry, while in the second half of the twentieth century, working class affluence grew.

Subsequent generations of women should be grateful that those days of coal-fired ovens, hip baths, cleaning maggot-ridden game and the scouring of chamber pots have gone from our society.[14]

There were as many different opinions of their time in service as there were interviewees, depending on their particular experiences.

EILEEN

They owned you. Once or twice, when they were going into Reading and it happened to be my half day they took me into Reading. But I had to sit in the car. I wasn't allowed to get out of it. I think they were afraid that I would run away. Looking back over the years, we were slaves, weren't we? What a cheek

---

[14] Frank Dawes *Not in Front of the Servants: Domestic Service in England 1850 – 1939*, Wayland Publishers, London 1973

to expect you to have that uniform; to wear the uniform and the colour they told you you had to wear. You had to buy it out of a pittance.

ANNIE

I enjoyed domestic service, in so far as I had had the seventeen weeks training and I knew what to do. Everything was what we call real wood in those days, solid oak, solid mahogany. Whilst I was there, every month was a special clean-up. There was no Electrolux or Hoover; it was just a carpet sweeper. You would have to roll the carpet up and take it out the back and put it on the line and beat it. Every month then, we'd have a little soapy water with vinegar in it, wring out the cloth until it was pretty well dry, wipe over all the furniture. That would take off all the old polish, then you'd start from fresh. It used to gleam; it was wonderful to see it. It really was lovely to see it.

There were very few regrets amongst my Welsh women. I did meet a lady at a history group meeting who told me that her grandmother used to say – 'I should have stayed! I should have stayed!' – She had been in service in Bath and came home to rural Monmouthshire which was very quiet after the excitement of fashionable Bath. All were very stoical in their recollections and final thoughts on their years in service. They had very modest ambitions for their lives if they had taken different paths:

MAY

I think if I was given the chance domestic science would have been my career. I used to love cooking. I took over when I came home to do the cooking for my mother.

MARGARET C.

I didn't go into service from choice. I would like to have been a teacher and I would have liked to have travelled. I love travelling.

EUNICE

I don't know if I would change anything, other than I would have liked to have been a domestic science teacher; whether I would have been good at it, I don't know. I'm quite happy with what happened really. I'm not bitter at all.

HAZEL

I would have liked to have stayed in the Forces if I had been able to. I could have become an officer, I think, eventually. I could have been a catering officer, because the opportunities were there. I don't regret my time in service. I was a bit of a rebel refusing to do a few things, but I also did that in the forces!

PHYLLIS

If my life had been different, I really don't know what I would have done. I loved children, so it would have probably been something with children, because I do really love children. I think as well, I'd like to look after elderly people. I think I would have the patience because I love old people.

HILDA

Looking back on my domestic service days, I really enjoyed it. I would say it opened a new life for me, to see how the other half lived, especially in the big house. Although they were gentry they were careful and they knew how to treat you. Some people say the rich have no consideration, but they did have consideration. I was very fortunate, in one way. I was able to handle those beautiful things and to live in that wonderful atmosphere, to live in an area with a deer park and lovely surroundings. I appreciated that very much. To go out and pick wild strawberries, in the woods, things like that.

ANNIE

I don't know what I would have done if I hadn't gone into service. I had no choice really, but I was quite brilliant on science. I knew everything about the atoms and the molecules.

Nobody in the class could touch me. Probably if I had had a chance, I would have gone on. I was very interested in science; I would have gone on there.

It was not unusual for the employer and the servant to become very fond of each other.

MARGARET C.

Anyway Mrs Ellwood came home eventually because her daughter wrote and told me she was in hospital, I think it was heart trouble. They weren't so clever in those days as they are now. And then she wrote and told me that her mother died. She would always write to me, see, and Miss Whitely. I don't really know what became of them; I often think about them. She was a really kind lady. She was very, very good to me. I'll never be able to repay Mrs Ellwood.

PHYLLIS

I went around looking for a job; they were two a penny. They loved to have the Welsh girls. I was looking and you meet one another and they recommend you. I got this job. I was part-time nurse-maid and part-time house work. She was a very nice person. They sold materials for dresses and that. They were very nice.

Dorothy also spoke of the popularity of Welsh girls in London, contrary to the findings of Margaret C.

People liked Welsh girls in London, they preferred Welsh girls. They found that they worked better than English girls. I know when I was in one job, with the Captain in the school, when we had to have another girl, he said, 'Get one from Wales now. They're better workers.' I did get one from Wales to come up.

Having listened to the stories of girls in service it would be fascinating, to hear the other side. How did the employers cope with these young Welsh girls? Were they aware of the homesickness, the conflicts below stairs, their loneliness and their pranks? The difficulty is that the employers are long gone. I have had one or two people approach me, in rather an embarrassed way, to say they remember girls working in their homes, when they were young too. My mother's family had a girl to live in when baby number four was born. There was twelve years' difference between my mother and her new brother so this girl was only a couple of years older than her. They remained friends all their lives and Bertha often came to tea with us when we were children.

A bank manager's daughter, I shall call her Jean, approached me after a meeting to tell me of the maids she remembered as a child. They had a series of them, some of them not lasting very long – 'flouncing off.' One maid used to look after her and her brother when her parents went out. She would entertain them by standing on her head. Her brother used to urge her to do it and then they would see her knickers – pea green directoire! The one that stayed the longest was called Vira, short for Elvira. She came from the Rhondda and was one of seven children. Her mother had died and although she was in the grammar school her father said she had to leave and earn her own living. She was fourteen when she came to work for them, the same age as Jean, who remembers her as a very quiet girl. She was with them until the War came when she joined the RAF.

Jean's mother, who had been a domestic science teacher before marrying, taught Vira cooking and they absorbed her into the family, although Jean can't remember talking to her very much or even going to the pictures with her. Jean does remember her father being very kind to her and helping her manage her money and opening a savings account for her, although Jean thought she only got about 12/6 a week. She had her own bedroom and was obviously very happy working for this particular family. Jean said, 'She was a very good companion for my mother.'

The collapse of domestic service, as an integral part of the social structure, finally all came together at once with the onset of better jobs outside the home and machines inside. The kitchen sink was

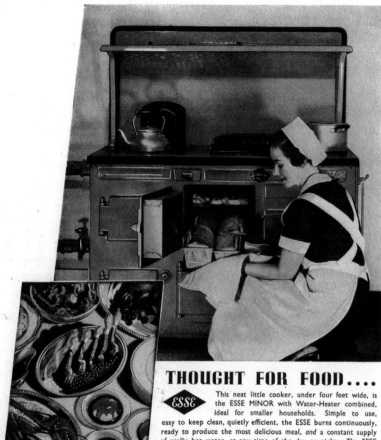

THOUGHT FOR FOOD....

ESSE This neat little cooker, under four feet wide, is the ESSE MINOR with Water-Heater combined, ideal for smaller households. Simple to use, easy to keep clean, quietly efficient, the ESSE burns continuously, ready to produce the most delicious meal, *and* a constant supply of really hot water, at any time of the day or night. The ESSE Heat-Storage Cooker is heavily insulated and will not over-heat your kitchen during the summer months.

Call and see a demonstration, or write for full particulars to Dept. P.23, at any of the addresses below.

ESSE Cookers are extremely economical and noted for fine cooking. Fuel : anthracite. Full particulars, including details of the PREMIER ESSE for large residences and the ESSE MAJOR for commercial catering, will be sent on request. Hirepurchase terms from elevenpence a day.

THE ESSE COOKER COMPANY

BONNYBRIDGE, SCOTLAND ● PROPRIETORS: SMITH & WELLSTOOD LTD. (Est. 1854)
WEST END SHOWROOMS AND DEMONSTRATING KITCHENS
63 CONDUIT STREET, LONDON, W.I. Central 3655 (6 lines)
Also at 11 LUDGATE CIRCUS, E.C.4, and at LIVERPOOL, EDINBURGH and GLASGOW

SOUTH AFRICA : Agents in all the leading towns. RHODESIA (Southern & Northern) : The S.A. Timber Co., Ltd., Corner Manica Road & Second St., Salisbury. AUSTRALIA : Anthony Hordern & Sons, Sydney, N.S.W. NEW ZEALAND : John Chambers & Sons, Ltd., P.O. Box 934, Auckland, with branches at Wellington, Dunedin, Christchurch & Invercargill. ARGENTINE & URUGUAY : Wilson, Sons & Co., 345 Calle Sarmiento, Buenos Aires. MAGALLANES : H. A. Cheyne, Magallanes.

The maid and the modern world in 1937.　　　　　(Advertising Archives)

abandoned for the typewriter, the shop counter and the factory bench. A ready and reliable source of electricity in our homes meant that whole ranges of machines were developed that could do the housework. Refrigeration resulted in daily shopping being no longer essential; central heating, replacing filthy coal fires, did not need constant attention; simple and dependable cookers were equally beneficial. Vacuum cleaners superseded carpet beating; laundry could be done by machines that became so sophisticated it could even be done in absentia and precluded the need to run in and out of the rain! There have also been enormous advances, both in textile and cleaning technologies, that have made our lives less tedious – terylene, drip-dry cottons, washing detergents – the list goes on.

In previous generations every cook had to undertake the heavy kneading of dough for bread-making and every household had to endure the steam and hard labour of the wash day. In the 1920s and 1930s bread and cakes came from the bakery and the washing went to a commercial laundry. Jams and ale were bought ready-made instead of being made at home by the servants. Little restaurants sprang up all over London, relieving domestic staff of the work of preparing a late dinner. More and more household tasks were being handed over to outside specialists.

Difficult economic times have now shifted from Wales to other parts of the globe and it is from these hard-pressed places that domestic staff for our hospitals, clubs, hotels and private homes will be found. We should consider the former experiences of our own young girls when faced with these migrants, often very young themselves, far way from their homes.

I have heard so many stories since embarking on this study and the one that brings tears to my eyes every time I repeat it is the one told me by a gentleman at a U3A meeting in Cardiff. His older sister was in service and worked for the family who manufactured HP Sauce, in Leamington Spa. As a little boy he went with his parents on a day's excursion to visit her. The host family kindly stayed in the garden so that the girl could show her parents around the house where she worked. The train bringing them home left Birmingham

New Street Station. The platform was lined with young Welsh people who worked in the Midlands, saying good-bye to their family and friends who had visited them. As the train drew away the youngsters broke into song and waved Welsh flags. Strains of 'Mae Hen Wlad Fy Nhadau', the Welsh National Anthem, could be heard above the sound of the departing train.

It is fitting, perhaps to end with a quotation from the autobiography of Elizabeth Andrews, who was the organiser of the Women's Section of the Labour Party in Wales, at that time. She wrote:

> When history comes to be written, about this period of
> mass unemployment, it will be dealt with in statistics and
> percentages. Readers and students of the future will need much
> imagination and understanding to give the human factor its
> rightful place.[15]

---

[15] With thanks to Honno Press for permission to reproduce the words of Elizabeth Andrews taken from *A Woman's Work is Never Done* introduced by Glenys Kinnock and edited by Ursula Masson, published by Honno Press in 2006 and available to purchase from www.honno.co.uk

Bibliography

Andrews, Elizabeth, *A Woman's Work is Never Done*, Honno, Wales, 2006

Beddoe, Deirdre, 'Women Between the Wars' in *Wales Between the Wars* Eds T Herbert & GE Jones, University of Wales, Cardiff, 1988

Beddoe, Deirdre, *Back to Home and Duty*, Pandora, London, 1989

Beddoe, Deirdre, '*Munitionettes, Maids and Mams: Women in Wales 1914-1939*' in *Our Mothers' Land* Ed Angela John, Cardiff University Press, 1991

Beeton, Isobel, *Book of Household Management*, Beeton, London, 1859

Burnett, J, *Useful toil: Autobiographies of Working People from the 1820s to 1920s*, Penguin Books, 1974

Constantine, S, *Unemployment in Britain between the Wars*, Longman, 1980

Davidson, Caroline, *A Women's Work is Never Done*, Chatto & Windus, London, 1982

Dawes, Frank, *Not in Front of the Servants: Domestic Service in England 1850-1939*, Wayland Publishers, London, 1973

Dyhouse, Carol, *Feminism & the Family in England 1880-1939*, Blackwell, Oxford, 1989

Ebery, N & Preston, B, *Domestic Service in the late Victorian and Edwardian England 1871-1914*, University of Reading

Evans, EG, *Spoken History*, Faber & Faber, London, 1987

Evans, Siân, *Life Below Stairs*, National Trust, London, 2011

Foley, Winifred, *A Child in the Forest*, BBC London, 1974

Giles, Judy, *The Parlour and the Suburb. Domestic Identities, Class, Femininity and Modernity*, Oxford, 2004

Giles, Judy, 'Home of One's Own: Women & Domesticity in England 1918 –1950' in *Women's Studies International Forum Vol 16 No.3*, 1993

Gittins, Diana, *Fair Sex: Family Size and Structure 1900-1939*, Hutchinson, London, 1982

Glucksman, Miriam, 'The Work of Knowledge and the Knowledge of Women's Work' in *Researching Women's Lives From a Feminist perspective* Eds Mary Maynard & June Purvis, Taylor & Francis, London, 1994

Goode, G & Delamont, Sara, 'Opportunity Denied: The Voices of the Lost Grammar School Girls of the Inter-War Years' in *Our Daughter's Land* Ed Sandra Betts, University of Wales Press, Cardiff, 1996

Harrison, Rosina, *The Lady's Maid; My Life in Service*, Ebury Press, 1988

Hawkesworth, John, *Upstairs Downstairs*, Sphere Books. London, 1971

Hopkin, D, 'Social Reactions to Economic change' in *Wales Between the Wars* Eds T Herbert & GE Jones, University of Wales Press, Cardiff, 1988

Horn, Pamela, *The Rise & Fall of the Victorian Servant*, Gill & MacMillan, Dublin, 1975

Horn, Pamela, *Women in the 1920s*, Amberley Publishing, Stroud 2010

Horn, Pamela, *Life Below Stairs in the Twentieth Century*, Amberley, Stroud, 2010

Hudson, Derek, *Munby: Man of Two Worlds*, Abacus Publishing. London, 1974

Keast, Moira, *The Story of Kayser Bondor*, Baldock Museum & Local History Society, 2007

Lewis, Jane, *Women in England 1870–1950*, Wheatsheaf Books, Sussex, 1984

Light, Alison, *Mrs Woolf and the Servants*, Penguin, 2007

Maloney, Alison, *Life Below Stairs*, Michael O'Mara Books Ltd, London, 2011

Musson, Jeremy, *Up and Down Stairs. The History of the Country House Servant*, John Murray, 2009

Powell, Margaret, *Below Stairs*, Peter Davies, London, 1968

Roberts, Elizabeth, *Women's Work 1840–1940*, Macmillan, London, 1988

Roberts, Robert, *Roberts' Guide for Butlers and Other Household Staff*, Applewood Books, Massachusettts, 1827

Rowbotham, Sheila, *Hidden From History*, Pluto Press, London, 1973

Sambrook, Pamela, *Keeping Their Place: Domestic Service in the Country House*, The History Press, Stroud, 2005

Staines, B, 'The Movement of Population from South Wales with Specific Reference to the effects of the Industrial Transference Scheme 1928–1937' in *Modern South Wales: Essays in Economic History* Eds C Barber & L J Williams, University of Wales Press, Cardiff, 1986

Swift, Jonathan, *Directions to Servants*, 1745

Taylor, Pam, *Women Domestic Servants 1919–1939*, University of Birmingham, 1976

Thomas, George, *Mr Speaker: the Memoirs of Viscount Tonypandy*, Century Publishing, London, 1985

Waterson, Merlin, *The Servants' Hall: A Domestic History of Erddig*, Routledge & Kegan Paul, 1982

Williams, Chris, 'Democratic Rhondda; Politics & Society 1885–1951', PhD Thesis, University of Wales, 1991

The Duties of Servants. A Practical Guide to the Routine of Domestic Service, Copper Beech Publishing, 1894

Appendix

1. A table listing the details of the 20 women interviewed by the author

NAME	D.O.B	PLACE OF BIRTH	OCCUPATION OF FATHER	SIBLINGS IN FAMILY	AGE WHEN FIRST AWAY	FIRST WAGE	PLACE OF FIRST POSTING	GENERAL FEELINGS
1. Dorothy	1907	Clydach Vale, Rhondda	miner	5	14	30s p/m	London	miserable
2. Mary K.	1908	Treorchy, Rhondda	miner	12	19	7/6 p/w	London	mixed
3. May	1913	Treorchy, Thondda	miner	10	14	7s p/w	Bognor	miserable
4. Phyllis	1913	Tylorstown, Rhondda	stoker in colliery	12	14	7/6 p/w	London	contented
5. Elizabeth	1914	Ynyshir, Rhondda	railway	6	14	£3 p/m	London	happy
6. Margaret C.	1913	Cardiff	seaman	6	14	4s p/w	Penally nrTenby	contented
7. Mary W.	1914	Wellington but came to Pontypridd as an orphan	miner	11	15	30s p/m	Dorset	mixed
8. Hilda #	1913	Ferndale. Rhondda	miner	7	17	£3 p/m	Surrey	mixed
9. Megan ~	1917	New Tredegar	miner	5	14	£1 p/m	Malvern	stoical
10. Eileen	1918	Aberkenfig, nr Bridgend	signalman in colliery	4	14	10s p/w	Reading	miserable
11. Ceinwen #	1918	Cefn Cribbwr, nr Bridgend	miner	13	14	£2 pm	London	scared
12. Morddfa	1914	Ogmore Vale	carpenter in colliery	12	19	7/6 p/w	London	happy
13. Nellie ~	1919	Newport	ironworks	5	14	4s p/w	Newport	mixed
14. Nancy	1919	Hednedsford, Staffs	under manager in colliery	3	14	7/6	Birmingham	happy
15. Miriam *	1918	Pontypridd	stonemason	9	16	10s p/w	Surrey	happy
16. Doris ~	1920	Treherbert, Rhondda	railway guard	2	14	7/6 p/w	Malvern	very happy
17. Margaret D. '	1919	Aberdare	haulier in colliery	2	16	5s p/w	London	happy
18. Hazel #	1923	Caerau nr Maesteg	miner but long term sick	5	14	6s p/w	London	content
19. Annie *	1923	Mountain Ash	unemployed council worker	9	14	£1 p/m	Cardiff	very happy
20. Eunice	1925	Caerphilly	railway, platelayer	4	14	5s p/w	Melksham	miserable

worked for gentry   *received formal training   ~ worked in institutions

2. A map of South-east Wales showing the birthplace of each woman respectively. Nancy was born outside Wales.

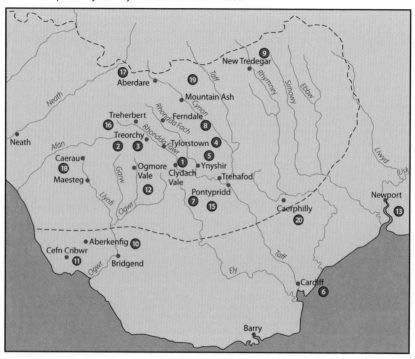

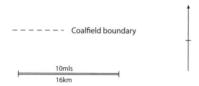

- - - - - - - Coalfield boundary

10mls
16km

3. A table comparing the respective wages earned by each of the women during their first year in service.

NAME	FIRST YEAR OF WORK	PLACE	POSITION	AMOUNT PER ANNUM	SENT MONEY HOME
1. Dorothy	1921	London	Kitchen maid	£18	£1 p/m
2. Mary K.	1927	London	General	£18.10s	Some
3. May	1927	Bognor	Children's maid	£18.4s	One third
4. Phyllis	1927	London	General	£18.10s	Doesn't remember
5. Elizabeth	1928	London	Kitchen maid	£48	10s p/m
6. Margaret C.	1929	Tenby	General	£10.8s	Half
7. Mary W.	1929	Dorset	Kitchen maid	£18	10s p/m
8. Hilda	1930	Surrey	Parlour maid	£36	Didn't ask
9. Megan	1931	Malvern	Kitchen maid	£12	16s p/m
10. Eileen	1932	Reading	General	£26	Half
11. Ceinwen	1932	London	Kitchen maid	£24	Paid for uniform
12. Morddfa	1933	London	General	£18.10s	Didn't ask
13. Nellie	1933	Newport	House maid	£12	No
14. Nancy	1933	Birmingham	House maid	£18	No
15. Miriam	1934	Surrey	Chamber maid	£26	no
16. Doris	1934	Malvern	House maid	£18	For saving
17. Margaret D.	1935	London	Cook	£13	Didn't ask
18. Hazel	1937	London	Kitchen maid	£15.9s	Half
19. Annie	1937	Cardiff	Cook's assistant	£12	No
20. Eunice	1939	Melksham	General	£13	no

Pre-decimalisation there were twelve old pennies in one old shilling (12d = 1s). Twenty old shillings in one old pound (20s = £1).

The value of money has changed so much that tables of equivalents should be consulted, e.g. Ceinwen's wages of £24 per annum would be equal to nearly £1,300 in 2013 prices. In other words her £2 per month would be equal to £100 per month, plus her board and lodgings.